UP BEFORE DAYBREAK

COTTON

AND

PEOPLE

IN

AMERICA

UP BEFORE

COTTON AND

DAYBREAK
PEOPLE IN AMERICA

DEBORAH HOPKINSON

SCHOLASTIC NONFICTION
AN IMPRINT OF
■ SCHOLASTIC

For Joy Folk Thomas, with love and admiration

Library of Congress Cataloging-in-Publication Data
Hopkinson, Deborah. Up before daybreak : cotton and people in
America / by Deborah Hopkinson. p. cm. Includes bibliographical
references and index. ISBN 0-439-63901-8 1. Cotton picking—
Social aspects—United States—History. 2. Cotton growing—Social
aspects—United States—History. 3. Cotton trade—Social aspects—
United States—History. 4. Slaves—United States—Biography.
5. Cotton farmers—United States—Biography. 6. Sharecroppers—
United States—Biography. 7. Textile workers—United States—
Biography. 8. Working class—United States—Biography. I. Title.
HD8039.C662U645 2005   331.7'63351'0973—dc22   2005008128

10 9 8 7 6 5 4 3 2   06 07 08 09 10

Printed in the U.S.A.   23   First printing, April 2006
Book design by Richard Amari
The display type was set in Lo-Type.
The text type was set in 10-pt. Mendoza Roman.

ACKNOWLEDGMENTS

A book is like a journey, and this one more than most. The two years in which I worked on *Up Before Daybreak* brought many life changes, and I owe a debt of gratitude to the family, friends, and colleagues whose support made it possible to complete this project.

I am especially grateful to Lisa Sandell for her skilled, gracious, and compassionate editorial guidance, to say nothing of her tireless pursuit of perfect photographs. Thanks also to Amy Betz for her encouragement, enthusiasm, and support of the original idea. Dr. Rebecca Sharpless, whose expert work in *Fertile Ground, Narrow Choices: Women on Cotton Farms of the Texas Blackland Prairie, 1900–1940*, served as an inspiration, read the manuscript, and offered valuable suggestions. I am grateful to Martha Mayo, Director of the Center for Lowell History at the University of Massachusetts–Lowell, for her insight into Lowell history and her generous reading of the manuscript. Thanks also to my agent, Steven Malk, and to the staff and librarians at the Lowell National Historical Park, the American Textile History Museum, also in Lowell, Massachusetts, and the Library of Congress, who were ever helpful.

My own journey has taken me far from Lowell. I owe enormous debts to my late parents, Gloria and Russell Hopkinson, to the late Kathleen Clark, to Robert Aitken, and to childhood teachers in the Lowell public schools who encouraged me along the way. Thanks to my sisters, Janice Fairbrother and Bonnie Johnson, and to Victoria Hemphill, who grew up with me in Lowell. So many dear friends were there the past two years to listen and support me, especially during long drives between Walla Walla and Corvallis. I don't have room to list you all, but from the bottom of my heart I send out special thanks to Maya Abels, Michele Hill, Deborah Wiles, and Anne Van Kley. And, of course, to Andy, Rebekah, and Dimitri — thank you for lighting my life.

CONTENTS

PART II

TOUGH TIMES

The Civil War and After

UNRAVELING
THE THREADS

Henry Kirk Miller never forgot the day the big freedom came. Henry was born into slavery on July 25, 1851. He was just fourteen in 1865, when the Civil War ended. From the time Henry and his sisters were small, the woman who owned them hired them out and kept the money for herself. Henry was sent to work on a cotton plantation about twenty miles away from the rest of his family. Then the war came, and with it, hard times. Henry's owner needed more money. She sold one of Henry's sisters and took cotton for pay.

"I remember hearing them tell about the big price she brought because cotton was so high," said Henry. "Old mistress got 15 bales of cotton for sister. . . . It was only a few days till freedom came and the man who had traded all them bales of cotton lost my sister, but old mistress kept the cotton."

Today, it's hard to imagine that America was once a place where children were traded for bales of cotton. It's also hard to imagine how one plant — cotton — could have played such an important part in the lives of millions of people like Henry and his sister.

The story of cotton — growing it, taking it to market, and making it into cloth — is like a thread that stretches far back into America's past. To understand how Henry's sister was sold for fifteen bales of cotton, we have to follow that thread back to the beginning.

Although I was born about a hundred years after Henry Miller, cotton shaped my world, too. I grew up in the old mill city of Lowell, Massachusetts, about thirty miles

A view of Lowell, Massachusetts.
AMERICAN TEXTILE HISTORY MUSEUM.

north of Boston. Today, it's the site of the Lowell National Historical Park, a museum that pays tribute to the place where America's Industrial Revolution began, and where generations of workers toiled in the textile mills.

Here you can ride in a boat along more than five miles of canals to see how the rivers provided power to the mills. You can stand in the open brick courtyard of the enormous Boott Cotton Mill and see the clock that called the laborers to work. You can hold a bobbin in your hand.

When you walk into the operating weave room you can even see — and hear — cloth being made. It's almost impossible to stand and listen for more than a few minutes in the middle of the eighty-eight clattering power looms without covering your ears. It's even harder to imagine working in this room from early morning until night, day after day, year after year.

When I was a girl in Lowell, there was no museum. I remember only a worn, faded town, shadowed by hulking brick buildings pitted with dirty and broken windows. Growing up, I never fully understood how important those old, run-down mills had been to our country's history. The evidence was right before my eyes, but I couldn't imagine the past. I couldn't see Lowell as a vibrant center of new technology or understand the forces that had left it broken and economically depressed.

Now, as I write, I have a single cotton boll in front of me. Hidden inside its soft fluffiness are small, hard seeds. Sometimes I try to pull one out. It's harder than you think — the fibers cling to it, and you have to work it this way and that. It's almost as if the cotton wants to hold on to it and keep it hidden.

In a certain way, telling the story of cotton and people in America has been like pulling seeds from a cotton boll. The story of cotton is the history of countless ordinary individuals, whose names, songs, hopes, and fears are, for the most part, lost to time. Enslaved children collecting shoefuls of cotton seeds before bed, mill girls pasting poems next to their looms, sharecropping families rising before dawn to spend long, torturous hours in broiling cotton fields.

Most of the people who speak in this book told their stories many years ago. The Lowell mill workers spoke to oral-history interviewers in the 1970s and 1980s. In the 1930s, workers in a program called the Federal Writers' Project interviewed former slaves. The Federal Writers' Project provided jobs for people during the hard economic times of the Great Depression. Although these interviews with former slaves give us insights into life in slavery times, as with any historical document, it's also important to understand how the interviews came to be.

For example, scholars today are careful about how oral histories are recorded. They try not to influence someone's story, put words into his or her mouth, or change the meaning. But most of the Federal Writers' Project interviewers weren't trained in oral history. They may not have all written down conversations in the same way. They might have edited the words or dialect. Most of the writers were white, interviewing blacks in the still-segregated South. Historians remind us that this in itself probably influenced what former enslaved people might have felt comfortable talking about.

Nevertheless, these interviews are a link with people who lived during slavery. While keeping the flavor of individual personalities and stories, I have edited the language to make it easier to read. The notes at the end of the book provide information on where to find the original interviews, many of which are available on the Internet.

The history of cotton is much too long and complicated to be contained in just one book. Yet I hope the stories, voices, and pictures in *Up Before Daybreak* will help readers begin to understand and unravel the powerful and often heartbreaking story of cotton and people in America.

Sorting cotton.

KING COTTON

Before the Civil War

"All hail to the great king...

Great King Cotton..."

— CIVIL WAR SONG, 1862

CHAPTER ONE

A SHOEFUL OF COTTON SEEDS

"Before they ever had a [cotton] gin, Master used to make us pick a shoe-full of cotton seeds out every night before we went to bed. Now that don't sound so bad, Missy, but did you ever try to pick any seeds out of cotton?"

— PAUL SMITH, former slave, Georgia

THE BEGINNINGS

On April 26, 1607, three ships from London crossed the stormy Atlantic to land on the shores of Chesapeake Bay. The ships carried English settlers to the new colony of Virginia. Right away the settlers planted gardens, carefully tending the vegetable seeds and young seedlings they'd carried so far. A month after their arrival, one settler reported back to London that these gardens were beginning to thrive, gardens that included orange trees, potatoes, pumpkins, melons — and cotton plants. As they minded their gardens, these early colonists could hardly imagine that cotton would become the single most important ingredient in America's economy before 1860.

Cotton didn't become the most important crop in America right away, however. Although Virginia colonists sent a sample of cotton they'd grown back to England in 1622, it took more than a century before cotton was grown for export. Even then, the amounts grown were somewhat small. About 43,000 pounds of cotton were shipped from Virginia to Great Britain in 1768, and Florida shipped nearly 22,000 pounds in 1780.

Woman with a spinning wheel.
AMERICAN TEXTILE HISTORY MUSEUM.

Before long, events occurred in Great Britain that would change everything. These changes became known as the Industrial Revolution.

INDUSTRIAL REVOLUTION: ENGLAND FORGES AHEAD

For centuries, people had produced goods by hand. But beginning around the middle of the eighteenth century in England, the invention of new, power-driven machines transformed how people lived and worked. At the heart of these changes was cotton.

Making and exporting cotton cloth had been an important part of the economy of England for many years. In the 1600s and early 1700s, merchants relied on the "putting out system" to produce cloth. In this system, farming families made extra cloth at home, which merchants would then buy to sell to people in many parts of the world.

But since this method of producing cloth was slow, it was hard to make a lot of money this way. English merchants were eager to find quicker, more efficient ways to produce cloth. To do this, they needed to invent machines that would make the work go faster, machines that would take the place of labor done by hand.

People, of course, had been making cloth by hand for centuries. In their search for clothing, people have always turned to materials close at hand, making creative use of plants and animals around them. Women had relied on spinning wheels and small hand looms to weave cloth and make clothes for their own families.

To make cloth from cotton takes several steps. First, fibers are separated from the plant. Then, dirt, leaves, and seeds are picked out from the fiber. Carding is a way to comb the fibers and join them into a sort of loose rope. Next, comes spinning, the process of drawing out and twisting together the fiber to make thread or yarn. The earliest spinning was done by hand, by twisting the fibers together. A stick can also be used. In drop spinning, a spindle — a rod or stick with a whorl or weight on one end — is used to twist the fibers into yarn. Spinning wheels allow spinners to make yarn more quickly. And, of course, using machines is fastest of all.

Once you have yarn, you can weave cloth. In weaving, yarn is wound on spools or reels called bobbins, which are loaded onto looms. On a loom, the yarns that run lengthwise are called warp yarns. Weft, or woof, is the term for the crosswise yarns that are shuttled back and forth across the warp to create woven fabric. It's easy to imagine that from field to fabric, making cloth by hand takes a lot of time and effort!

When people invented new machines and found ways to harness water and steam power, they completely transformed how cloth was made. Now something that for centuries had been done in the home could be mass-produced in factories. Today, it's hard to really grasp what a big change this was for Western society. The truth was, though, that the change from producing items by hand to using power-driven machines created a revolution. It changed not just what people could buy, but it changed how and where people lived and what jobs they did. It led to new ways of life and new problems, too. It's no wonder that this seemingly simple change from

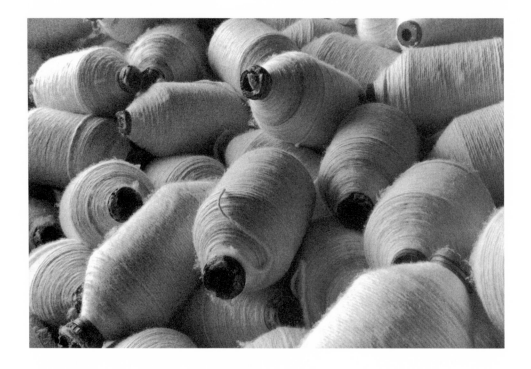

hand-produced goods to those produced by power-driven machines is called a revolution — the Industrial Revolution. And it began with cotton.

Several English inventors played key roles in inventing machines to make cloth from cotton as well as wool and other fibers. To mechanize the spinning process, in 1764, James Hargreaves introduced the spinning jenny, an early form of spinning machine that had several spindles. The spinning jenny used a wheel that the spinner operated using both hand and foot. A few years later, in 1769, Richard Arkwright invented a water-powered spinning frame that helped to speed up the spinning process. By the late 1780s, more than one hundred mills in England had adopted this kind of machine.

In 1779, a man named Samuel Crompton invented a "mule," a combination of the jenny and frame machine, which could make different sizes of yarns, suitable for different thicknesses of cloth. The first models carried 48 spindles, but by 1800, mules powered by steam held more than 250 spindles, and by 1835, 1,000. At about the same time, in 1785, power looms were invented. Improvements on the looms continued to be made into the nineteenth century. To get an idea of how fast the textile industry grew, consider this: In 1765, about a half million pounds of cotton were spun into yarn in England by hand. Twenty years later, that number had risen to *sixteen million pounds* — all spun by machine!

These inventions fueled the growth of the textile industry. Mills mushroomed in English towns and cities. And as the textile industry expanded, it needed more cotton.

THE PROBLEM OF SEEDS

Cotton has been around for a long time. A shrubby plant, it thrives in warm climates in many parts of the world. Historians believe that Neolithic farmers first began to grow cotton for its seeds and fiber about ten thousand years ago. Archaeologists have found evidence of cotton production and early cotton gins in Asia, Africa, South America, and by Native Americans in what is now the American Southwest. Written accounts of cotton grown in India date back to the fourth century B.C.

Today, there are around fifty different species of cotton. About four of these are grown for seed or fiber. Cotton is a perennial, but it's normally treated like an annual, so cotton seeds usually need to be planted each year. Its fruit, about the size of a golf ball, is called a boll.

Although the cotton boll is a fruit, it can't be eaten. Instead, when it matures, it opens in four sections to reveal a soft, white fiber — a downy ball of fluff. About fifty seeds are embedded inside this dense fiber.

Of course, to use this soft cotton fiber, the seeds have to be taken out. Certain kinds of cotton, called long-staple cotton, have smooth seeds that are easily removed. But the varieties of cotton that grew best in most parts of the American South are a different kind, called short-staple or fuzzy-seed cotton, because the seeds have a fuzzy covering.

Cotton bolls. AMERICAN
TEXTILE HISTORY MUSEUM.

If you hold a boll of fuzzy-seed cotton in your hand and squeeze, you can feel the tiny bumps of seeds inside. But when you try to get the seeds out — watch out! It's tricky. The cotton fiber sticks to them. It's a little like trying to pull stickers off your socks after you've been for a walk in a field or getting burs out of the thick coat of a dog.

For generations, people have struggled to find the best way to remove the seeds from cotton fiber quickly and easily. On small farms, women who wove cotton for their families often depended on their children to help.

A woman named Katy Williams once told her daughter that when she was a small child in Texas, she had to pick the seeds from cotton every night. "The task set for them was that there should be enough seed to fill the child's shoes," Katy's daughter recalled years later. "This made enough cotton for grandmother to card, spin, and weave the next day. . . ."

Pulling the seeds out by hand might work for a small amount of cotton. Yet by the end of the eighteenth century, the Industrial Revolution was making the mills of England hum. England couldn't grow cotton itself. The climate was too cold for this heat-loving plant. The British were already importing cotton grown in India and in the islands of the Caribbean. But the hungry mills demanded more. American planters who wanted to grow more cotton still had to face the problem of extracting those tiny seeds. Until, that is, the problem was solved.

THE COTTON GIN

The cotton gin was invented to separate the seeds from cotton and has existed for centuries. In places like India, cotton gins similar to those made in the fifth century were still in use in the late twentieth century. This gin features an iron roller and a flat base. The person operating the gin leans over the base, grasps the ends of the roller, and rolls it over the seed cotton (cotton and seeds together), pinching the seeds out of the cotton fiber. This cotton fiber is also sometimes called lint.

As we have seen, in the latter part of the eighteenth century, the British textile industry was beginning to create a demand for more cotton. In the 1770s, as American planters began growing more fuzzy-seed cotton to export to England, they relied on several different varieties of roller gins to clean the cotton before putting it in bales to be shipped.

Cleaning cotton with these gins was a painstaking process. Paul Smith, a former slave from Georgia, recalled, "Those home-made cotton gins were mighty slow. We never saw fast store-bought gins in those days. Our old gins were turned by a long pole that was pulled around by mules and oxen, and it took a long time to get the seeds out of the cotton that way."

Then, in 1794, a man named Eli Whitney invented a new form of gin altogether. Originally from New England, Whitney was living near Savannah, Georgia, in 1792, when he began to tackle the problem of removing seeds from cotton. Whitney was a talented mechanic. Instead of using a roller that pinched off the fiber, he developed a gin with coarse wire teeth that stripped the cotton lint from the seeds by pulling it through a narrow grid or grating too fine for the seeds to pass through. He obtained a patent for his invention in March 1794. A few years later, a mechanic from Georgia

An early cotton gin.
LIBRARY OF CONGRESS.

named Hodgen Holmes improved Whitney's model, using an axle with fine-toothed saws. Holmes received a patent for his model in 1796.

Whole books have been written about the cotton gin and its inventors. But simply put, over time, the gins based on Whitney's "toothed" or "saw-toothed" model have come to be known as "saw" gins, as opposed to the earlier "roller" gins.

The saw gin became popular immediately. It was simple enough to be built in an hour by a carpenter. And it could gin cotton more quickly than roller gins. The saw gin was developed at the right time for American planters, just, as we have already seen, when the Industrial Revolution in England was exploding, and the demand for cotton was greater than ever before.

Because of this, planters throughout the American South were eager to produce more cotton and grasp this chance to make money. But growing cotton was hard work, all of it tedious, brutal, and time-consuming. Planters and landowners didn't want to do this difficult work themselves.

The planters wanted a cheap labor force, field hands to do the backbreaking toil of growing and harvesting cotton. In the South, enslaved African people became that labor force. Cotton and slavery went hand in hand.

CHAPTER TWO

UP BEFORE DAYBREAK: COTTON AND SLAVERY

"Everybody had to get up before daybreak. . . ."

— RICHARD ORFORD, former slave

SARAH'S STORY

I sure have had a hard life," Sarah Gudger declared. "Just work, and work, and work. I never knew nothin' but work. I never knew what it was to rest. I just worked all the time from mornin' till late at night."

Sarah Gudger was born into slavery. When Mrs. Gudger was interviewed in 1937, she said she'd been born in 1816, which would have made her 121 years old! Although no one can be certain of Mrs. Gudger's true age, all the evidence at the time showed she was indeed more than one hundred when she told her story.

By then, Mrs. Gudger was living in Asheville, North Carolina. She stood about five feet tall, walked with a crutch, and had short white hair. Despite her age, Sarah Gudger hadn't forgotten the harsh treatment she'd suffered so many years before. When asked about what her life had been like under slavery, Mrs. Gudger held out her arms and crossed her wrists to show how her hands had been tied before being whipped.

"Old Master strapped us good if we did anything he didn't like. . . . Sometimes he got his dander up and then we daren't look round at him," she said. "Or else he'd tie your hands 'afore your body and whip you, just like you're a mule. . . . I've taken a thousand lashings in my day. Sometimes my poor old body was sore for a week. . . ."

African Americans prepare cotton to be ginned at a South Carolina plantation. THE GRANGER COLLECTION.

Sarah Gudger, a former slave, was interviewed for the Federal Writers' Project.
LIBRARY OF CONGRESS.

Sarah Gudger remembered how she worked until late at night, whatever the weather. In the cold rain her clothes stuck to her body. "I had to card and spin [cotton] till ten o'clock. Never got much rest, and had to get up at four the next mornin' and start again. Didn't get much to eat, either, just a little corn bread and molasses."

COTTON AND SLAVERY

Slavery in America didn't begin with cotton. The first enslaved Africans were brought to Jamestown, Virginia, in 1619. At first, these slaves worked mostly on tobacco plantations.

As the Industrial Revolution increased demand for cotton, planters along the Georgia and Carolina coast began growing the long-staple variety of cotton, with its smooth black seeds that could be separated by hand. But this kind only grew well in a few places. After Whitney's gin was invented, though, planters could grow short-staple varieties and use saw gins to separate the cotton fiber from the seeds. From then on, cotton spread more rapidly, and by 1820, it was being grown not just on the coast, but inland as well. By the 1840s, it had spread across the South, reaching as far west as Texas.

Cotton production in America grew very rapidly during the 1800s. Poor white farmers eking out a living on small farms might also grow some cotton as a cash crop. Larger plantations relied heavily on enslaved workers to clear the land, break up the soil, "chop" (or thin) the young cotton plants, pick tufts of fiber from prickly bolls, separate the seeds from the fiber, pack the fiber into bales, and load the bales onto wagons and boats. Enslaved people built America's cotton empire.

In 1800, fewer than one hundred thousand bales of cotton were produced in the South. By 1860, on the eve of the Civil War, four million bales of cotton were grown. These four million bales made cotton the most important export in the United States before the Civil War. Known as "King Cotton," this one crop truly ruled.

Many people made money as the cotton industry grew, but not the people who worked hardest at bringing those four million bales to market. The astounding growth of the cotton industry would not have been possible without the labor of

Planting cottonseed.
LIBRARY OF CONGRESS.

three million enslaved men, women, and children — three-quarters of the Southern slave population — who toiled day after day in the fields.

BEFORE IT WAS LIGHT

It took a lot of labor to export four million bales of cotton. And it wasn't just adult slaves who were forced to give their lives to cotton. Children were enslaved, too. And they worked hard.

Richard Orford was born into slavery on the Georgia plantation of Jeff Orford. Like other slaves, Richard had no rights. He wasn't allowed to go to school or learn to read and write. Richard or any member of his family could be sold away at any time. He couldn't travel freely, control his own future, or own property. Even Richard's last name came from his master.

Picking cotton was backbreaking work.
LIBRARY OF CONGRESS.

In 1847, when Richard began working in his master's house, he was only five. Every day, Richard had to keep the yard clean and feed the chickens. By the time he was eight, he was driving the mistress around in a carriage. Richard worked for the master and mistress in the "Big House." But most of the other 250 slaves on the Orford plantation spent long hours in the fields.

"Even before it was light enough to see, they were in the fields waiting to see how to run a furrow," Richard remembered. "Long about nine o'clock breakfast was sent to the fields in a wagon and all of them stopped to eat. At twelve o'clock they stopped again to eat dinner. After that they worked 'till it was too dark to see. Women in those days could pick five hundred pounds of cotton a day with a child in a sack on their backs."

At age eighty-seven, John Walton, who'd been born August 15, 1849, in Austin, Texas, could still recall his boyhood as a slave in the cotton fields of Bill Walton's plantation. "Even us kids had to pick 150 pounds [of] cotton a day, or get a whoppin'. I put the cotton in the white-oak baskets and some of them held more than 100 pounds. . . ."

DAILY LIFE, CLOTHES, AND FOOD

What was it like to be a child on a plantation? Paul Smith was born on Ellis Plantation in Oglethorpe County, Georgia. Paul and his family were owned by Jack and Lizzie Ellis. Paul recalled how the seasons governed everyday life.

"Along about the first of March, they took the pants away from all the boys and gave them little shirts to wear from then 'til frost. Those shirts were all us boys had to wear in summer 'til we were big enough to work in the fields," said Paul. "Gals jus' wore one piece of clothes in summertime too; they wore a plain cotton dress. All our clothes, for summer and winter too, were made right there on that plantation. They wove the cloth on the looms; plain cotton for summer, and cotton mixed with a little wool for winter."

A drawing of a slave cabin.
LIBRARY OF CONGRESS.

David Wilborn, born in Athens, Georgia, in 1856, was the son of a Cherokee father and a mixed-race mother. After the Civil War, he became the first black undertaker in Dayton, Ohio.

"Of course we lived in a cabin. That was the way all slaves lived. We ate corn bread and fat meat, and hardly any vegetables, and syrup," he said, recalling his boyhood. "We went barefoot, and wore loose shirts with a hole cut out for the head to go through, and a hole for each arm. Many a day I picked cotton from sunrise to dark when I was just a little fellow."

The work itself was hard enough, but the brutality of owners and overseers caused even more misery. John Walton remembered one rough overseer who forced workers, even children, to keep up with the leaders. If they couldn't, the overseer would "ride up and down and hit us over the back if we didn't do the job right. Sometimes he'd get off his horse and have two slaves hold one down and give him the bullwhip."

HANNAH SCOTT'S STORY: I NEVER KNEW MY OWN PA

"I never knew my own pa," said Hannah Scott, a former slave from Alabama. "He belonged to another man and was sold away before I was old enough to know him."

Hannah's first master, Clark Eccles, owned nine slaves. Hannah remembered her first master and mistress as kind. But kindness didn't change the fact that Mr. Eccles owned Hannah's family. And when Mr. Eccles got into debt, he sold his slaves to a man named Bat Peterson, who put Hannah and her family in a wagon and took them to Arkansas.

Life on Bat Peterson's plantation was much harder for young Hannah. Instead of just a few slaves, here there were one hundred, along with two black drivers and an overseer. Hannah's new master "was mean, too, and worked his slaves from daylight till nine o'clock at night."

As a young girl, Hannah's job was to carry water into the fields for the workers. "I carried the bucket on my head and before long I didn't have any more hair on my head than you have on the palm of your hand," she said.

"When I got bigger, the overseer put me in the field with the rest. Master Bat grew mostly cotton and it don't make no difference if you were big or little, you better keep up or the drivers burn you up with the whip," Hannah recalled. "Sometimes I got so tired come night, I dropped right in the row and went to sleep. Then the drivers would come along, and wham, they'd cut you across the back with the whip and you woke up, yes, sir!

"About nine o'clock they'd holler, 'cotton up' and that was the quitting signal," Hannah said. Many nights she was so tired, she simply dropped off to sleep without anything to eat.

"On old Bat's place that was all we knew, work and more work. The only time we had off was Sunday morning, and then we had to wash and mend clothes," Hannah said. On the first Sunday of each month a white preacher would come, but Hannah recalled that all he preached was obedience to the white folks, and "we heard enough of that without him telling us."

In this drawing, a slave carries a basket of cotton on his head. LIBRARY OF CONGRESS.

Once, after Hannah and her family had been in Arkansas five or six years, something surprising happened. Mr. Eccles, her old master, arrived to try to buy the family back. Hannah and her family wanted to go back to a place where at least they had been treated kindly. But it was not to be. "Old Bat wouldn't let us go. He come to our quarters that night and told Mama if she or us children tried to run off he'd kill us. . . . That's the way it was 'till we were freed."

By then, though, her master had moved west, to Texas, searching for new, better land for his cotton. "He thought if he brought us to Texas he wouldn't have to set us free. But he got fooled, 'cause a government man came and told us we were free," explained Hannah. Like Bat Peterson, many other slaveowners moved to Texas, hoping to keep their slaves in bondage for as long as possible.

Enslaved people had no voice in where they lived. In the early years of slavery, most slaves lived along the southern coast of the Atlantic. As time went on, and cotton plantation culture moved westward, through Alabama, Mississippi, Louisiana, Arkansas, and beyond, the lives of enslaved men, women, and children changed. Like Hannah, slaves were often torn from family and community.

Slavery began in America in the early 1600s and continued for more than 250 years. Slavery made some people poor in ways it is difficult for us to imagine today. It made others rich and powerful. And cotton was at the heart of slavery.

CHAPTER THREE

MOUNTAINS OF COTTON

"It must be seen to be believed . . . acres of cotton bales standing upon the levee . . . piled up in miniature mountains . . . boats are constantly arriving, so piled with cotton that the lower tier of bales on deck are in the water; and as the boat is approaching, it looks like a huge raft of cotton bales, with the chimneys and steam pipe of an engine sticking up out of the center."

— SOLON ROBINSON, New Orleans, 1848

COTTON! COTTON! COTTON!

On farms and plantations throughout the South, the hard work of cotton picking usually began in August. After weeks of harvest, the cotton was ginned and compressed into bulky, heavy bales. James Johnson, a former slave who worked in the cotton business in South Carolina after the Civil War, knew firsthand the danger of handling those cotton bales.

Loads of cotton gathered from the fields. LIBRARY OF CONGRESS.

"I have worked in the cotton business, first as a ginner and then with cotton buyers. . . . I know all the grades of lint cotton and can name them right now," Mr. Johnson told a visitor when he was seventy-nine years old. "I never seen a bale of cotton I couldn't pick up and tote where I wanted to, by myself. You see these feet of mine? They were

Kids sitting in a truck loaded with cotton. BUTLER CENTER FOR ARKANSAS STUDIES.

A cart carrying bales of cotton. LIBRARY OF CONGRESS.

mashed off, from droppin' bales of cotton on them, back yonder many years ago."

It's no wonder Mr. Johnson's feet were in bad shape — bales of cotton usually weighed between four and five hundred pounds!

Once the cotton was harvested, ginned, and compressed into bales, growers and plantation owners had to get the crop to market and sell it. In an age before trucks, railroads, or airplanes, the best way to transport hundreds of heavy cotton bales was by river. Once the cotton was sent to a port city, it would be loaded onto ships. Before the 1820s, most of the cotton grown in America was sent across the Atlantic to be processed by the new, power-driven machines in England's growing textile industry.

The rivers that connected the villages, farms, and towns of America created a vital network of trade. In America's early years, farmers used flatboats to send their goods downriver to markets. After 1807, when Robert Fulton invented the steam engine, steamboats made trade possible both upriver and down. To continue the river network farther, people built canals. In 1825, when the Erie Canal was completed, water travel from the Great Lakes in the Midwest to New York City became possible for the first time. It's no wonder that New York grew into the nation's center of commerce by 1860.

Like farmers in the North, cotton growers in the South relied on rivers to get crops to market. After the cotton was ginned to remove the seeds, then compressed into bales, it was usually stored on farms until fall rains made nearby rivers high enough to be navigable.

Boat landings and wharves dotted the riverbanks. Often these sported warehouses filled, of course, with cotton. When a steamboat arrived, heralded by the blast of a whistle or the firing of a gun, people flocked to the river to watch slaves load the steamboat with bale after bale of cotton.

New Orleans was a major shipping port for cotton.
LIBRARY OF CONGRESS.

On rivers such as the Apalachicola and Chattahoochee, which run through Georgia, Alabama, and Florida, most cotton was shipped between December and June. Thanks to these rivers, the Gulf of Mexico port city of Apalachicola, Florida, was a busy place. In 1840, 55,000 bales of cotton passed through the city. By 1853, that number had grown to 140,000 bales. Other ports grew just as fast. Much of the cotton was sent to Liverpool, England.

Warehouses overflowed, and bales of cotton spilled out onto the sidewalks. The streets were alive with cotton men. In fact, the whole city had the air of a bustling anthill, "where the ants were hurrying back and forth getting their food stored away for the winter." Cotton was the life of the town.

The numbers tell the story behind the mountains of cotton piled on the wharves. In 1793, America exported 2,000 bales of cotton, all to Great Britain. In 1860, the year before the Civil War began, America exported more than *3.7 million bales*, most of them to Great Britain.

Growing, selling, or buying cotton dominated the lives of people living in this river valley, as it did in other river systems of the South, such as the Alabama, Mississippi, and Savannah. Like cotton yarns, the rivers tied everything together, making the business of cotton possible — and profitable — for white businessmen and plantation owners.

THE BUSINESS OF COTTON

On April 22, 1853, a white Arkansas cotton planter named John W. Brown arrived in the bustling port city of New Orleans by steamboat. Mr. Brown was there on business, and the most important person he had come to see was Mr. Henderson, his cotton factor.

A cotton factor was a person whose job combined many things. He was a banker and a bookkeeper. He also helped his clients do business. During Mr. Brown's four-day stay in New Orleans, Mr. Henderson, his cotton factor, would probably introduce Mr. Brown to other businessmen, such as cotton buyers. The men would discuss the price of cotton or tour cotton warehouses.

A planter often borrowed money from the man who was his factor. If Mr. Brown needed to buy tools, supplies, groceries, or meat for his family and the slaves on his plantation, Mr. Henderson would pay all the bills. At the end of the season, once Mr. Brown's cotton crop had been sold, he would repay the money he'd borrowed.

The cotton factor also sold the grower's cotton crop. The factor worked to find a buyer. At first, most cotton grown in America was shipped in bales to England to be made into cloth in the textile mills there. By the time Mr. Brown was growing cotton, in the middle of the nineteenth century, cotton was also being shipped north to mills in New England. For their services, cotton factors such as Mr. Henderson were

The inside of a cotton warehouse. LIBRARY OF CONGRESS.

usually paid a commission of 2.5 percent of the total amount that the planter received for his cotton.

While many cotton factors lived full-time in port cities like New Orleans, others, such as young John Chrystie of New York, came to Apalachicola, Florida, just for the winter cotton season, setting up shop in one of the many brick warehouses lining the waterfront. Not only did John work in a warehouse, he lived there, too.

"We have a large three story brick warehouse in the rear of the second floor of which are two rooms — one is the counting room and immediately adjoining is our sleeping room, Harry and myself," John wrote home to his family. "This is very convenient as we can be as late and as early at business as we please. We feed at the hotel where we have as good a table as we ever sat down to. . . . In the evening we sit in our offices and play whist, or read papers when they come or write letters."

In his job as a clerk for a cotton factor company, John Chrystie was very busy. In one week, he might have to arrange for seven or eight thousand bales of cotton to be loaded onto ships. In a time before e-mail, phones, or computers, he wrote twenty or thirty business letters each day by hand.

FAIR TO MIDDLING: PRICING COTTON

Once the planter's cotton crop arrived in the warehouse, the cotton factor checked the quality of the cotton. He needed to check its color and how clean it was, so he looked for dirt, twigs, and leaves. All this helped determine the price he'd be able to get for the cotton.

The cotton was examined in the sample room, which was usually in the front part of the warehouse. David Black, who worked with cotton in Georgia, explained, "A place must be selected where the greatest amount of light would fall on the tables where the cotton samples were classified. The grade and the initials of the owner are indicated on a slip of paper and rolled inside of the sample."

Clean cotton with a creamy tint was the best, while dull white cotton was worth less. The worst was "spotted" or "tinged" cotton, which had turned brown because of frost or insect damage. Gray cotton had been exposed too long to rain, fog, or dust. Each bale of cotton had to be looked at and marked.

After the samples were taken, the cotton factor wrote to the planter to tell him how much the planter might expect to get for his crop. Sometimes the news wasn't what the planter wanted to hear.

"We put the samples on the boards today and in a more careful examination find we were mistaken when we valued the crop at $10\frac{1}{2}$ to $10\frac{5}{8}$ [cents per pound]," wrote one factor to a planter in March 1859. "The crops from the neighborhood of your plantation appear to have been injured by the storm in September. They are dingy in color and more trashy than usual."

THE WHEELS OF FORTUNE

On September 30, 1844, a newspaper reporter in the port of Apalachicola, Florida, announced the beginning of cotton season. In a few weeks, he wrote, the steamers would be "booming down the river with their tall chimneys just peeping over the bales of cotton . . . our wharves will be covered with cotton — our streets filled with people, and the places of business and amusement opened and every inducement held out to those who wish to enter the field of competition and struggle on for wealth. . . . Onward and onward will roll the wheels of fortune."

In 1844, sixty-two ships entered Apalachicola Bay from New York alone. Other

---

GRADES OF COTTON

The color and the length of the cotton (long fibers were more valuable), along with how much debris was in the cotton as it was ginned, determined the grade of each cotton bale. Middling cotton was the basic grade. There were thirteen grades in this order, from best to worst:

Fair

Strict middling fair

Middling fair

Strict good middling

Good middling

Strict middling

Middling

Strict low middling

Low middling

Strict good ordinary

Good ordinary

Strict ordinary

Ordinary

Unloading cotton from a riverboat. LIBRARY OF CONGRESS.

American boats arrived from Mobile, Charleston, New Orleans, Baltimore, Rhode Island, Massachusetts, and Maine. Foreign vessels hailed from Cuba, Liverpool, the West Indies, Jamaica, Marseilles, and the Virgin Islands. In the 1842–1843 shipping season, 105,934 bales of cotton were exported out of Apalachicola.

Besides being cotton factors, white men worked as bankers, mill owners, official cotton weighers, and shipowners. Insurance agents covered the risk of fire while cotton was being transported or stored. Lawyers collected overdue debts. Companies whose names are familiar today trace their roots to this time: insurance agents such as Aetna, and the credit-rating agency R. G. Dun and Company, forerunner of Dun and Bradstreet.

Many people had jobs related to cotton. During the 1800s, the South continued to focus more and more on cotton, creating a profitable industry, built, of course, on the labor of slaves.

Cotton could not be grown in the North, because the climate was too cold. But in the early nineteenth century, cotton would find its way to New England just the same. As it had in England, the textile industry would launch the Industrial Revolution — this time in America.

CHAPTER FOUR

AT THE CLANG OF A BELL:
THE MILL GIRLS OF LOWELL

"I shall not stay here. . . . Up before day, at the clang of a bell and out of the mill
by the clang of the bell — just as though we were so many living machines."
— ANONYMOUS MILL GIRL, Lowell, Massachusetts

COTTON IN THE NORTH: LUCY'S STORY

So far, most of the cotton story has taken place in the American South. And it's easy to understand why. By the early nineteenth century, all the pieces needed to make cotton king in the South were falling into place.

English mills were demanding more cotton fiber, just as the invention of the saw gin made removing cotton seeds from fiber more efficient than ever before. Southern plantation owners wanting to grow more cotton in their warm climate used slaves to do all the hard, brutal field work. After it was harvested and ginned, cotton was sent in large bales down southern rivers to ports such as New Orleans. From there, it was shipped across the Atlantic Ocean to English mills, to be made into cloth.

In the 1830s, however, the North began to play a larger role in the cotton industry. As these changes took place, cotton came to touch the lives of many ordinary men, women, and children in the North as well as the South. One person who became part of this changing world was a girl named Lucy Larcom.

A New England mill girl.
AMERICAN TEXTILE HISTORY MUSEUM.

Lucy Larcom, after working in the Lowell mills, graduated from the Monticello Seminary and became a teacher and poet. PEABODY ESSEX MUSEUM.

Lucy Larcom was born in Beverly, Massachusetts, in 1824, thirty years after Eli Whitney invented his new kind of cotton gin. One of her earliest memories was seeing the stars for the first time. She remembered being lifted up under the dark, still, clear sky, thick with stars. Lucy was amazed to realize that this bright sky was the roof over the big house she lived in — Earth.

Lucy's memories of her first years were full of stars, wildflowers, birds, and the wonders of the sea. She loved to roam the sandy beaches near her Beverly home and gather seashells in her apron.

One of eight children of Benjamin and Lois Larcom, Lucy often tagged along when her older brother, John, picked huckleberries. Sometimes they took long walks, stopping at brooks to hear the catbirds sing or on the beach to listen to the chant of the waves.

Lucy was a dreamer who loved nature, poetry, and books. Work was another matter. She would much rather snooze under the apple trees listening to birds than weed her father's garden! Lucy didn't care much for sewing, either, and her first efforts at making a patchwork quilt ended in disaster. Her sisters laughed and teased her, calling her attempts at sewing "gobblings."

Although the Larcom children often played in the nearby graveyard, death didn't seem real to them. But that changed when Lucy's father died. Her mother was now a widow with eight children. She faced pressures and problems Lucy couldn't begin to understand.

In 1832, there were few paths open to Lucy's mother. Unable to survive in the countryside, she decided to take her children away and make a fresh start. She decided to run a boardinghouse for young women who worked in the new cotton mills that were being built on the banks of the Merrimack River.

When the Larcom family arrived in Lowell in 1832, they were among the first wave of Americans seeking their livelihoods in cotton mills. As we know, growing and shipping cotton was already big business in the South, but America lagged behind England in the actual production of cotton cloth in mills using machines such as spinning mules and power looms. In other words, while power looms were being used in English mills as early as the 1780s, these inventions hadn't yet come to America's shores.

Although some cotton-spinning mills had begun to appear in the United States around the turn of the eighteenth century, most were small operations. Samuel Slater opened the first cotton-spinning mill in Pawtucket, Rhode Island, in 1790. Nine children, ages twelve and under, worked there. But while spinning was done in the mill, Slater hadn't figured out how to build a power loom. Once the yarn was spun, the cloth still had to be woven *outside* the factory, by women and men in their homes. In the following years, more small spinning mills dotted the New England countryside, but none were on the scale of English mills.

But Northern businessmen were watching the English textile industry closely. After all, there was a supply of cotton in the South. Why shouldn't America be able to both grow cotton and produce cloth? But no one in the United States had yet figured out how to build the machines, like the power loom, that were being used in England.

Then one man solved the puzzle. In 1814, Francis Cabot Lowell built a small mill on the Charles River in Waltham, Massachusetts. Lowell's mill was the first in America to handle the total production of cotton cloth — carding, spinning, and weaving — just like the mills with power looms operating in England since the 1780s.

How was Francis Cabot Lowell able to accomplish this? A few years before, in 1810, Lowell had visited textile mills in England. Lowell was excited by what he saw. He looked at everything closely, trying to memorize the designs of these new machines built to spin and weave. This couldn't have been easy, since the English manufacturers wanted to keep the designs secret to guard against competition.

Lucy hated to leave the woods and fields she loved, and her little patch of garden with its lilacs, peonies, and the morning glories she'd planted. But the day came when Lucy took the first stagecoach journey of her life to a new town. The town, like Lucy, was young and growing fast. As Lucy stood outside her new empty house, watching for the big wagon loaded high with her family's household things, she couldn't know that someday her name would be memorialize in her new home — Lowell, Massachusetts.

A NEW KIND OF FACTORY

"In the sweet June weather I would lean far out of the window, and try not to hear the unceasing clash of sound inside. . . . I loved quietness. The noise of machinery was particularly distasteful to me. . . . And I defied the machinery to make me its slave. Its incessant discords could not drown the music of m thoughts if I would let them fly high enough."

— LUCY LARCO

Upon his return, with the help of a mechanic named Paul Moody, Lowell was able to accomplish something extraordinary: the "re-invention" of the power loom used in England. Lowell then went on to design a factory that could handle the entire process of transforming bales of cotton into cloth — right here in America.

Lowell's invention launched the beginning of the Industrial Revolution in America. Now America could compete with England in textile production. America would be able not just to grow cotton but to spin it into yarn and weave it into cloth in American mills. This new American textile industry could produce cloth for its own people and for export to other countries.

Unfortunately, Francis Cabot Lowell didn't live long enough to realize the significance of his new mills. He died in 1817, when he was only forty-two. But his name will always be linked with the birth of American industry.

An illustration showing a woman working at a power loom. AMERICAN TEXTILE HISTORY MUSEUM.

In 1821–1822, several Waltham mill investors and friends of Lowell's decided to undertake a grand experiment. They would build a new city along the Merrimack River in Massachusetts, taking advantage of the waterpower of the river's Pawtucket Falls. Through the use of machines and waterpower, the new textile mills would handle the total process, from cleaning raw cotton to the weaving of cloth.

These investors hoped this new city would become the country's largest center of industry, with mills, houses for workers, shops, and parks. They dreamed of creating

something new, a "city of the future, the wonder of the nation," and they named it Lowell in their friend's honor.

MILL GIRLS

Back in 1814, when the Waltham mill first opened, word quickly spread throughout the countryside that the mill promised jobs — jobs for young women. And when the mills of Lowell opened their doors almost ten years later, farm girls throughout New England flocked to the new city, eager to work.

Some, like Lucy Larcom, had been forced to leave the countryside. Others simply wanted to escape the dreary hard work and loneliness of farm life. They yearned for independence, their own money, and a more active social life.

Laura Nichols from Connecticut wanted to earn her own money. She hoped to get more education, but her parents couldn't afford to help her. So Laura took a job in a mill near her home, determined not to give up her hopes for the future.

Years later, Laura told her own children how hard she had been willing to work for her dreams. Laura believed there was "something better within my reach and I must have it or die in the attempt. I began to realize that my future would be largely what I made of it, that my destiny was, as it were, in my own hands."

New England girls like Laura were part of a new chapter in American history. The early years in Lowell and the other mill towns of New England marked the first time large numbers of women moved away from their families to cities to take jobs far from home.

By 1840, there were about ten major companies operating more than thirty textile mills in Lowell. Powered by water from the Merrimack River, the mills were enormous brick structures standing five or six stories tall. Some employed as many as 1,800 workers. Brick boarding-houses for single women and men who worked in the mills lined nearby streets, while married men with families often lived in brick town houses.

Mills dominated the city's life: By 1840, 9,500 women and men worked in Lowell's textile mills, about 50 percent of the city's total population. More than

An advertisement calling for young women to work in the Lowell mills. BAKER LIBRARY, HARVARD BUSINESS SCHOOL.

75 Young Women

From 15 to 35 Years of Age,

WANTED TO WORK IN THE

COTTON MILLS!

IN LOWELL AND CHICOPEE, MASS.

I am authorized by the Agents of said Mills to make the following proposition to persons suitable for their work, viz:—They will be paid $1.00 per week, and board, for the first month. It is presumed they will then be able to go to work at job prices. They will be considered as engaged for one year, cases of sickness excepted. I will pay the expenses of those who have not the means to pay for themselves, and the girls will pay it to the Company by their first labor. All that remain in the employ of the Company eighteen months will have the amount of their expenses to the Mills refunded to them. They will be properly cared for in sickness. It is hoped that none will go except those whose circumstances will admit of their staying at least one year. None but active and healthy girls will be engaged for this work, as it would not be advisable for either the girls or the Company.

I shall be at the Howard Hotel, Burlington, on Monday, July 25th ; at Farnham's, St Albans, Tuesday forenoon, 26th, at Keyse's, Swanton, in the afternoon; at the Massachusetts' House, Rouses Point, on Wednesday, the 27th, to engage girls,---such as would like a place in the Mills would do well to improve the present opportunity, as new hands will not be wanted late in the season. I shall start with my Company, for the Mills, on Friday morning, the 29th inst., from Rouses Point, at 6 o'clock. Such as do not have an opportunity to see me at the above places, can take the cars and go with me the same as though I had engaged them.

I will be responsible for the safety of all baggage that is marked in care of I. M. BOYNTON, and delivered to my charge.

I. M. BOYNTON,

Agent for Procuring Help for the Mills.

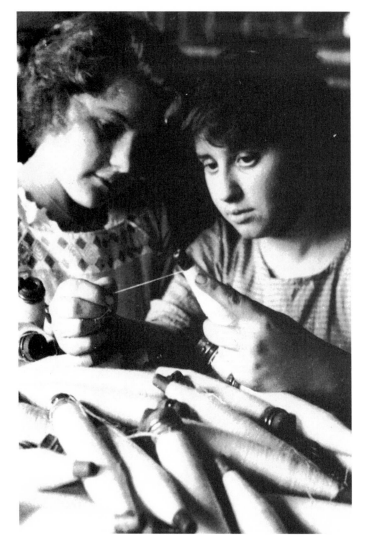

Young girls with bobbins.
AMERICAN TEXTILE HISTORY
MUSEUM.

half the women in Lowell worked in the mills.

On summer mornings, the mill bells would clang at four thirty, to wake workers throughout the city, then again in twenty minutes to call people into the mills. Work was six days a week, beginning at five A.M. sharp. At seven, the bell rang for a forty-five-minute breakfast break, followed by bells for the forty-five-minute noon break. People resumed their work from a quarter to one until seven in the evening, when the mills closed. At ten at night, the curfew bell rang.

Women in the mid-1830s earned about $3.25 for a seventy-three-hour work week — less than five cents an hour. But room and board was only $1.25 a week, so most women had $2.00 a week to call their own. And although the hours seem long, women living on farms also worked from morning until night.

NOT THE RIGHT SORT OF LIFE FOR A CHILD

In Lowell, Lucy helped her mother run the boardinghouse before and after school. Lucy made beds, trimmed the wicks of the oil lamps, and washed dishes. But money was still tight. When Lucy was eleven, her mother could no longer support the family without all her daughters going to work. So, like the young women who were her mother's boarders, Lucy Larcom, a girl who loved nature and sunshine, became a mill girl, spending day after day inside a hulking brick factory.

At first, Lucy went to work in the mill with a light heart. She was eager to help her mother. And the work seemed easy enough. Young as she was, Lucy had soon mastered her job as a doffer. A doffer was the person responsible for changing bobbins.

"It really was not hard, just to change the bobbins on the spinning frames every three-quarters of an hour or so, with half a dozen other little girls who were doing the same thing. When I came back at night, the family began to pity me for my long, tiresome day's work, but I laughed and said, 'Why, it is nothing but fun. It is just like play.'"

When she wasn't needed for changing the bobbins, Lucy played with the other girls, ducking in and out of the spinning frames and talking to the older girls who worked on them. Sometimes the overseer allowed Lucy and her friends to explore other parts of the factory.

Lucy never cared much for the noise of the machinery. "The buzzing and hissing and whizzing of pulleys and rollers and spindles and flyers around me often grew tiresome." But she couldn't help being impressed when she was allowed a peek at the great wheel that harnessed waterpower for the mill. "It was so huge that we could only watch a few of its spokes at a time," she said.

Lucy returned to school after about a year of work and was soon ready for high school. "But alas! I could not go. The little money I could earn — one dollar a week, besides the price of my board — was needed in the family, and I must return to the mill," Lucy later recalled. "It was a severe disappointment to me, though I did not say so at home."

Looking back, Lucy wrote, "The mill itself had its lessons for us. But it was not, and could not be, the right sort of life for a child."

Lucy made up her mind to go back to school someday. She'd always loved to write poetry, and she thought she would like being a teacher, too. And so, during the next several years, as she worked in the spinning room, Lucy determined to learn all she could.

THE *LOWELL OFFERING*

Women posing by wending spools at a mill in Connecticut.
AMERICAN TEXTILE HISTORY MUSEUM.

Mill girls weren't allowed to bring books into the mill. So Lucy Larcom pasted poems she wanted to memorize near where she stood all day. Lucy wasn't the only young woman in Lowell interested in self-improvement. Lowell offered lectures, evening classes, reading rooms, and circulating libraries. And the mill girls eagerly took advantage of these opportunities.

With her sister Emilie, Lucy joined other girls in a group they called "The Improvement Circle." By the early 1840s, there were at least seven similar clubs in Lowell. A young minister named Abel C. Thomas began to publish the girls' sketches, letters, and poems in 1840. In 1841, the publication became the *Lowell Offering*, a thirty-page monthly magazine, which sold for about six cents an issue. Another publication, called the *Operatives' Magazine*, which also began in 1841, was edited by two mill girls. In 1842, the two publications merged as the *Lowell Offering*, with two longtime mill workers, Harriet Jane Farley and Harriott F. Curtis, serving as editors.

The *Lowell Offering* achieved almost instant popularity and fame. It was published for five years, ending in 1845. In 1847, Harriet Farley resumed publishing this magazine in Lowell under the title *New England Offering*. This ended in the early 1850s when Farley moved to New York City to write, and where she eventually married.

CHANGING TIMES

New England women dominated the textile workforce in Lowell until the mid-1880s — when the workers were about 50 percent Northerners, 30 percent French Canadian, and 20 percent Irish.

Like Harriet Farley, many of the early Lowell mill girls eventually left their jobs to go back home, get married, or attend school, or sometimes because they were ill. Some went west as teachers, or entered new colleges for women. Laura Nichols, who had always dreamed of getting an education, quit her mill job when she had saved fifty dollars. She then left home to enroll in what is now Mount Holyoke College. Laura became a teacher and later traveled to Africa as a missionary with her husband.

Laura, Lucy, and other girls were replaced by several generations of young Northern women and men and some immigrants. Some were French Canadian, while others came from Ireland, fleeing poverty and famine at home. Still, it wasn't until after the

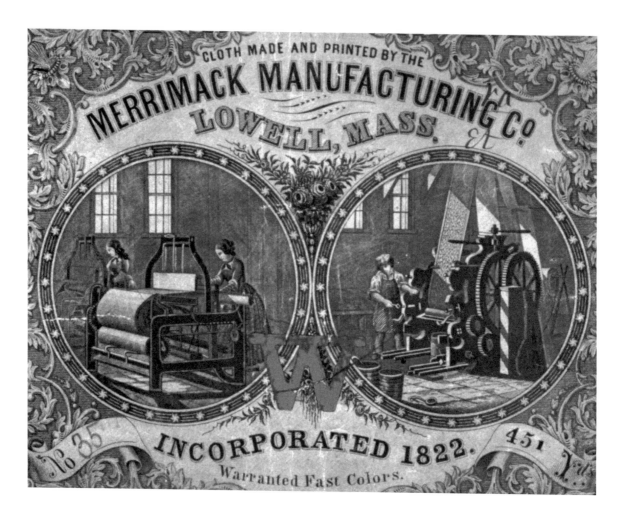

Civil War, in the 1880s, when vast numbers of French Canadian workers arrived, that the majority of textile workers in the Lowell mills were immigrants.

An engraving advertising the Merrimack Manufacturing Company. AMERICAN TEXTILE HISTORY MUSEUM.

In the years before the Civil War there was some improvement in working conditions for mill workers. For instance, while in 1839 workers toiled seventy-three hours a week, in 1853 that was reduced to sixty-six hours a week. Pay increased slowly, and safety conditions, machinery, and ventilation improved. But this didn't always translate into easier lives for immigrant workers, who were often married with children and struggling to support large families on textile-mill wages.

BIRTH OF THE AMERICAN LABOR MOVEMENT

The girls and women who came to the mills from farms and villages throughout New England had never had formal jobs before. They lived at a time when women were discouraged from taking a public role. The investors in the mills presumed that these young women would be agreeable workers and would be easy to manage. When the mill girls began speaking up for themselves on work issues, their activism surprised their families, mill owners, and the public.

Between 1824 and 1837, at least twelve strikes occurred in American textile mills in which women were the main participants. In 1836, about 1,500 Lowell female workers went on a successful rent strike, forming the "Factory Girls Association."

As one historian has noted, these women were "pioneers in the struggle for women's equal pay and equal rights in the workplace . . . and their efforts helped give birth to the American labor movement." Although these women lost many of their battles, they also won some, including several reductions in hours of work between 1847 and 1871. And, in 1874, the Massachusetts Legislature passed the first ten-hour workday for women and children in the nation.

As for Lucy Larcom, just as she had dreamed, she returned to school, then went on to become a teacher and poet. Today, she is still remembered in Lowell, where a small park is named in her honor.

CHAPTER FIVE

FROM CAN TO CAN'T: SHARECROPPERS AND TENANT FARMERS

"Picking goes on each day from can to can't. . . ."
— JAMES AGEE, 1936

THE CIVIL WAR

The Civil War is one of the most pivotal events in American history. It changed much: The country was not the same after the war as it had been before. Because of this, it's natural for scholars and historians to think of the Civil War as a dividing line in our past, just as the Civil War divides this book.

Many books have been written about the complex causes of the Civil War, causes beyond this story. But as you might guess by now, it's impossible to talk about the Civil War without talking about cotton.

By 1860, cotton dominated the American economy. And no wonder. The South exported 66 percent of the world's supply, and cotton made up more than half of all goods exported from the United States. Almost 90 percent of cotton grown in the South was exported, and the New England mills were just a small piece of the South's market. Much of Southern society had become dependent upon a cotton culture and the institution of slavery. In 1850, there were more than 74,000 plantations that raised five or more bales of cotton. The majority of these plantations were in Alabama, Georgia, Mississippi, and South Carolina.

A little boy picking cotton.
GETTY IMAGES.

Throughout the 1800s, cotton had made the South and the North very different regions. While the South had become a rural region of cotton farms and plantations, the North was becoming a more industrial region, with textile mills (which, of course, depended on Southern cotton), canals, railroads, larger cities, and a growing population of immigrants.

During the nineteenth century, tensions and disagreements between these two regions, especially over the spread of slavery, increased. Southern growers were interested in expanding the cotton culture westward. But cotton would not be profitable without slave labor. So they claimed. However, unlike Southerners, most Northerners were against slavery spreading to new American territories in the West. Yet the North depended on the cotton economy, too. The textile mills of the Northeast produced about $100 million worth of cloth, and sold it not only throughout New England and the expanding West, but to other countries and the South, as well.

While people tried to hold the Union together by making compromises, in the end, conflict over slavery and other key issues eventually erupted into war, which threatened to break the United States in two. Sometimes called the War Between the States, the Civil War began on April 12, 1861. It lasted for four bloody years, claiming an estimated 620,000 lives, until the North defeated the South.

Slavery had made cotton profitable. But the Civil War brought about the end of the institution of slavery. Would it also mean the end of cotton? And how would it change the lives of people who had worked in those cotton fields of the South and the textile mills of the North?

NO REAL MONEY: THE SHARECROPPING SYSTEM

By the time the Civil War ended in 1865, much of the South lay in ruins. Many farms and plantations had been burned. Hundreds of thousands of men had been killed or

Freed slaves turned sharecroppers. LIBRARY OF CONGRESS.

KING COTTON
CIRKUT PHOTO, COPYRIGHT 1907
BY J.C. COOVERT. 63 N.MAIN, MEMPHIS

wounded. People had to struggle to find ways to feed and clothe their families and rebuild their lives.

Plantation owners who'd been able to save some cotton during the war were in the best position. They could make a fresh start by selling what cotton they had and using the money to buy food, clothes, tools, and more cottonseed. Poor white farmers who had grown vegetables and cotton before the war had a harder time getting back on their feet and rebuilding their lives. Most had to borrow and use credit to buy the food, clothing, seed, and tools they needed right away. Some couldn't manage to scrape by. Many lost their small farms and had to go work for someone else.

Freedmen, or newly freed slaves, had the hardest time of all. Not only did they face hostility and prejudice from whites, but without money or an education most were forced to turn to landowners — their former owners — for the means to make a living.

Cotton had driven the economy before the war, and so it was natural that the people who had benefited most from cotton wanted to continue growing it. To do so, they needed to replace slaves with other labor. And since there were few other opportunities, most freed blacks and many poor whites had little choice: They had to work cotton, whether they wanted to or not. For these and other reasons, the system of sharecropping took hold in the South after the Civil War and remained in place until well into the twentieth century.

In sharecropping, owners divided their land into small plots tended by families who were paid a share of the crop. White landowners, who had the most money and land, did the best in this system. Tenant farmers, who owned their own tools and mules but farmed on someone else's land, were usually the next well-off. Tenants typically paid the landowner a third of their corn crop and a fourth of their cotton crop. This was sometimes called "farming on thirds and fourths."

Sharecroppers were even poorer than tenant farmers. Since they didn't even own tools, they depended on credit from merchants or landlords to supply everything from seed to mules. They usually split the crop down the middle with the landowner.

This was called "farming on the halves." Because of their debts, these families often ended up with nothing left over at the end of each harvest. Below sharecroppers were farm laborers, who got minimal wages. Some worked seasonally, while others performed odd jobs on the farms year-round.

STAY ON OR STARVE

Blacks might have been free from slavery, but sharecropping offered little hope for a future. A former slave named Ambus Gray explained how the system worked.

"You go up to a man and tell him you and your family wants to hire for next year on his place," Ambus Gray said. "He say, 'I'm broke, the war broke me. Move down there in the best empty house you find. You can get your provisions furnished at a certain little store in the closest town about.'"

The child of a black sharecropper working in the fields. LIBRARY OF CONGRESS.

After the crops were harvested, said Ambus, "about all you got was a little money . . . to give the man what run you and you have to stay on or starve or go get somebody else to let you share crop with them."

Like many sharecroppers, Ambus moved often from farm to farm, looking for a better situation. Ambus Gray was lucky. Through his hard work during "cotton boom times," years when crops were good and the price for cotton was high, Ambus Gray was eventually able to buy his own home. He paid one hundred and fifty dollars for it.

But most sharecroppers weren't able to break out of the system the way Ambus Gray did. Since store owners and landowners charged high interest rates on purpose, families were forced to live from harvest to harvest. If they *did* get cash after selling their part of the cotton crop, they had to use it to pay their debts. So then they had to start all over again, borrowing money to get by until the next year. Sharecropping families often sank deeper and deeper into debt. It was hard to escape the cycle of poverty.

IT TOOK ALL I HAD

Ned Cobb's father was a strict, harsh man who put Ned to work in the fields from the time he was just nine years old. One day after the harvest, when Ned was plowing down the leftover cotton stalks, "All of a sudden a stalk broke and flew back in my eye and knocked me out from between them plow handles."

Before long, Ned's eye was "just a lump of blood" and though the boy could not see out of it for more than a week, his father never took him to the doctor.

When Ned grew up, he became a sharecropper, too. But no matter how hard he tried, at the end of the year he only had enough to pay his debts to the white landowner.

"What did I have left? Nothin'," Ned declared. "You want some cash above your debts; if you don't get it you lost, because you gave that man your labor and you can't get it back."

As an African American, Ned Cobb faced even more obstacles than poor white farmers. The men he worked for often tried to control him and had no confidence in Ned's own abilities. Ned had to fight prejudice day after day.

Ned described his white landlords' attitude toward him this way: "You ain't got sense enough to know this, you ain't got sense enough to know that, you ain't got sense enough to know nothing. . . . I had to go by his orders to please him."

Ned soon realized that planters only cared about getting paid themselves. Keeping sharecroppers poor and in debt simply helped them replace the slave labor they'd lost. Black sharecroppers might have been free in name, but they were still bound to an oppressive system.

This white planter, Ned concluded, "ain't goin' to let me rise."

MY HOUSE IS SO ROTTEN: LIVING CONDITIONS

Living conditions were harsh for poor cotton farmers, white and black, who often lived in unimproved shacks or former slave cabins. One sharecropper said, "My house is so rotten you can jest take up the boards in your hands and cromple 'em up."

A Texas tenant farmer named Mr. Campos complained that his kitchen "has no ceiling. There is one wooden window. The roof is not much good. . . . The water has to be gotten from the river, 300 yards away." Tenants like Mr. Campos discovered that if they tried to fix up their houses, their landlords would just raise the rent.

Many of the houses in which cotton farmers lived had changed little since the days of slavery. Sometimes large families crowded together in tiny, three-room shacks. In the 1930s, one observer described seeing "unpainted weather-beaten houses where cotton is planted so near to the house that it is possible to stand on the door step and touch the plants. About some of these houses there are discarded boxes and rusty tin cans with flowers growing in them. To grow them has taken water. The many loops of rope at the well or the long path to the creek tell a pathetic story of the labor cost for the short lived beauty of these flowers."

Manuel Longoria, a Hispanic sharecropper in Texas, said that the tools his land-lord provided were practically useless. Then, when Manuel asked for credit to buy some clothing for his family, his landlord refused to give it to him unless Manuel agreed that the landlord would take his horse if he couldn't pay the money back.

"We can't get any flour, snuff, shoes, sugar, coffee, thread or anything from the

landlord but meat and meal," reported another farmer. "We have a devil of a time. No soap, soda, or salt. Can't borrow a dime, not a . . . cent. If this ain't hell, I'll eat you. We work our . . . heads off and get nothing. The harder we work, the deeper in debt we get."

Cotton families in rural central Texas and in many parts of the South had no electricity until the late 1930s. Houses were lit with kerosene or coal-oil lamps. In parts of central Texas, less than a third of white families and only 2 percent of black families had water in the house or on the porch in the 1920s. By 1940, only 16 percent of white tenants had running water in their houses, and fewer than 2 percent of black tenants did. Likewise, many of these families didn't have flush toilets or washing machines. Clothes were washed outside in tubs and hung inside and outside on bushes or fences to dry. In addition to long hours of chores at home, African American women often did laundry for others to help support their families.

Although they worked on the land, sharecropping and tenant farmers had a difficult time growing their own food. Instead, landowners and merchants wanted them to grow cash crops like cotton or tobacco, which could be sold for high prices. The result was that people didn't usually raise enough vegetables for their own

A white sharecropper's daughter. LIBRARY OF CONGRESS.

families to eat. Many children went hungry, or ate very unhealthy foods, which they bought at high prices from local stores.

Sharecroppers' diets revolved around the "three M's," that is: meat (fat salt pork), meal, and molasses. One study showed that pork, chiefly fat salt pork, made up 40 percent of the food of Southern tenant farmers. Since families moved often, even if they had extra money, they couldn't plant fruit trees that might take several years to produce.

Diets based on pork, cornmeal, and molasses syrup were high in fat, protein, and carbohydrates, but lacked essential vitamins and nutrients. In the early 1900s, a disease called pellagra

A sharecropping family in the fields. LIBRARY OF CONGRESS.

was common in epidemic proportions in the South and Texas. The disease affects the skin, the digestive tract, and the brain. Since corn lacks certain essential nutrients, such as niacin, pellagra is common in areas where corn is the main staple. Eventually scientists discovered the causes of pellagra and were able to prevent it by enriching corn products.

I HAD TO BE BOY AND GIRL

In sharecropping and tenant-farming families, both boys and girls worked in the cotton fields, but girls in families without brothers had extra chores. Because there weren't enough boys in Lydia Domasch's family in Fayette County, Texas, she had to help both her mother and father. "I had to fix lunch and bake bread the night before. In the morning we had a mile and a half to walk to the field. When I came home from the field, I had to pick up the eggs in the dark."

Eunice Austen was the oldest of four girls on a North Carolina farm. "I had to be boy and girl. I had to do work that a boy would ordinarily do, because my daddy didn't have any other help to do that. I hauled hay and shocked wheat and just anything. . . . I would always help plant the crop and do a lot of hoeing. Daddy just depended on me."

SCHOOL CAME SECOND

"I've sure had to work hard for all what's come to me ever since I got big enough to handle a hoe," said George Tanner, a tenant farmer in South Carolina, in 1939. "My mother died when I was a infant, and I lost my father when I was 'bout twelve year old. . . . I was forced to get out and hunt my own way of getting along, so I stayed from house to house and worked like a dog for other people.

"I don't remember ever going to school a day since I've been born," George reflected. "But education's a good thing and something everybody ought to have. I feel like I've missed half my share in life."

George Tanner's experience was common: School often came second to cotton. Planting cotton took place each spring, and harvest from August through November. Sometimes schools simply closed during harvest, even if the state laws required children to be in school. These "crop vacations" or "cotton vacations" interrupted children's learning year after year. The lack of education kept generations of families trapped in poverty and the sharecropping system.

In 1942, a man named Charles Gibbons spent several months collecting information about more than four thousand children in farming families in Missouri. Almost all the children he interviewed said that they picked cotton for one reason: to help their families.

Most of the children used the money they earned to buy things their families desperately needed: clothes and shoes, a piece of furniture, or a new roof. Sometimes they helped their families buy livestock, pay for an operation, or even assist with funeral expenses for a loved one.

Two brothers told Mr. Gibbons that they had earned enough money picking cotton to buy their mother a washing machine. Why was that important? Well, before that, one brother had been staying home from school every Monday to help his mom with the laundry. By chipping in to buy a washing machine, the boys wouldn't have to miss one day of school every week.

Girls work in the cotton fields.
LIBRARY OF CONGRESS.

Because so many schools in Missouri closed for cotton picking, in 1940, the state ranked thirty-fourth in the nation in school attendance. Charles Gibbons believed the only way to free children from "the curse of cotton" was for communities to make sure all children attended school. But, he wrote sadly, "Most of the local people have simply quit trying; cotton has been too much for them."

HOLDING ON

In the decades after the Civil War, the system of sharecropping kept generations of Southern families in poverty. The Cotton Belt, said one writer, was a "miserable panorama of unpainted shacks, rain-gullied fields, straggling fences, rattle-trap Fords, dirt, poverty, disease, drudgery, and monotony that stretches for a thousand miles."

In 1937, Erskine Caldwell and Margaret Bourke-White published a collection of photographs and text about the Southern system of sharecropping entitled *You Have Seen Their Faces*. Like the 1941 book *Let Us Now Praise Famous Men*, with text by James Agee and photographs by Walker Evans, *You Have Seen Their Faces* focused national attention on the harsh poverty resulting from sharecropping.

Caldwell wrote, "The tenant farmer in the South is trying to hold on to a spinning world until by some means he is enabled to get a grip on a better way of life. He knows he cannot buy land of his own from the profits of sharecropping. He knows . . . he cannot save until he earns, and that he cannot earn much more than a bare living from sterile, barren land.

"He does well . . . to hold on at all."

THEY CALLED US LINTHEADS:
MILL VILLAGES
OF THE SOUTH

"If we don't starve, nobody will,

Can't make a living in a cotton mill."

— FROM "COTTON MILL COLIC" BY DAVE McCARN, 1926

THINGS HAD GOT TOUGH

Flossie Moore Durham was born on a small farm in North Carolina around 1883. When Flossie was ten, her father died, leaving behind a wife and eight children.

There wasn't much money. "We lived; we never went hungry, we never went cold," Flossie said, recalling the hardships her mother faced. "But I've often wondered how she kept us all a-going."

Flossie's mother had to answer the same difficult question that Lucy Larcom's mother had, fifty years earlier. How could she make ends meet and take care of her children?

Like Lucy Larcom's family, Flossie's family decided to leave the countryside. Flossie and her family moved to Bynum, North Carolina, near the Hall River, where a new cotton mill had been built in the early 1870s. Flossie's life changed. Before, she had picked cotton. Now, she got a job in a mill spinning it.

———

Southern mill boys. LIBRARY OF CONGRESS.

MOVING TO A MILL VILLAGE

The mill village where Flossie lived was something new in the South. Before the Civil War, most of the cotton grown in the South had been shipped to mills in England or to the North. But although farming was still the main occupation in the South after the Civil War, people had also begun looking for other ways to improve the South's economy. One of those ways was to build more cotton mills.

New mills soon sprouted up, especially in the Piedmont, an area of rolling hills from southern Virginia through the central Carolinas into Georgia and Alabama. Here, as in New England, rushing rivers could provide waterpower for mills. In

The floor of a Mississippi cotton mill. LIBRARY OF CONGRESS.

North Carolina, about six new mills were built each year between 1880 and 1900; by 1900, there were 177 mills. Building mills in the South had some advantages. Rather than send cotton north, mill owners could make it into cloth close to where it was grown, saving shipping costs.

Families made the move from farming to mill work for many reasons. Some, like Flossie's family, moved when someone died or because crop prices fell very low. Sometimes their land was worn out. Others wanted to escape from being tenant farmers or sharecroppers.

"Things had got tough in the country," declared Alice Harden. "Farming, where you rented, was getting difficult to make a living. That's the reason we moved to the mill."

Alice and her siblings liked mill work better than farming. At the mill village, the family got jobs and a house. "We thought it was easier. We had more time to do what we wanted." But for her father it was different, Alice remembered. "I don't think my father liked it at all, because he had rather be on the farm."

Like Alice Harden's father, John Wesley Snipes, a North Carolina cotton farmer, hated to leave the country. He hung on, working rented land, for as long as he could. In good years he sold his cotton for about forty cents a pound. But then the price dropped to four or five cents a pound, so instead of getting $200 for a five-hundred-pound bale of cotton, he was only able to sell it for $25 a bale. Between poor prices and the loss of his plants to insects, Snipes was finally forced to admit defeat — he couldn't clear even a dime. John Snipes and his wife moved to Bynum and began working in the cotton mill.

People didn't leave their farms all at once. But from the 1870s through the 1930s, many white families like the Hardens and the Snipeses gave up growing cotton or left small farms where they'd been eking out meager livings raising grain and corn, and tending cattle and hogs. First to move were widows and single women and female laborers in the 1870s and 1880s, followed by families headed by men in the late 1880s and 1890s after prices collapsed and poor soil, depleted by growing cotton year after year, could no longer support the farms. Landowning and tenant-farm families alike turned to the mills.

A second mill building boom in the early twentieth century attracted more people. Josephine Glenn and her husband tried to support their four children on shares until the mid-1930s. "As soon as the Depression came on, there just wasn't anything on the farm, especially for sharecroppers, and we didn't have our own home. We started working in the mill," she said.

For Josephine, it wasn't a matter of choice. "I had four little reasons" — her children.

When Southern farmers left the land and took a cotton mill job they called it "public work." Most were earning hourly wages for the first time in their lives.

A textile worker named Joseph Michaels remembered that the mills also recruited workers. "Long hours and low wages made it hard for mills to get hands, and to keep them. Most mills had labor agents, they called them, slave

Girls take a break from work outside a Georgia mill. LIBRARY OF CONGRESS.

dealers would have suited better, and these labor agents traveled through the surrounding country searching for tenant families that were in hard luck. If a bad crop year had caught them, or if death or sickness had struck."

Mills offered some choices to struggling whites, but most blacks were barred from Southern mill work. When African Americans were hired, it wasn't for production jobs, where workers could increase their pay as they gained skill and speed. Instead, black men worked in the mill yard, moving heavy bales of cotton, or doing the tedious, dirty work of cleaning cotton when it arrived at the mill. Black women also faced harsh employment discrimination and usually could only find janitorial jobs such as sweeping or cleaning bathrooms.

Shelby Kirk, an African American woman from Landis, North Carolina, had picked cotton on land her father rented for as long as she could remember. Shelby was a married teenager with children when she went to work cleaning in a cotton mill.

A young girl walks through a Mississippi mill village.
LIBRARY OF CONGRESS.

"This man come down here one evening and said that a boss man in the cotton mill had told him to find four black women to work in the mill," she recalled. "So he came down here and asked me and three other women if we would go and try to work in the Collier Mill, and that's where we found a job. . . . Miss Ethel and myself were the first black women to work in the mill in Landis."

IN THE MILL VILLAGE

"I was born up in Banks County, my folks owned a big farm up there. After Dad died there was nobody to work it, and Mamma wanted to come to the cotton mill," remembered Estelle Berry, a white mill worker from North Carolina.

"We lived in a cotton mill house on the factory hill,"

Estelle went on. "The rent wasn't much, because the people can't afford to pay much rent out of what they make. This house had a bath and electric lights, and it cost us four dollars a month."

Estelle had to quit school in second grade to look after her ill little brother. She did most of the family's cooking and cleaning. The whole family looked forward to payday. Her mother would "put on a clean frock, then we'd all go to the store. The main things like flour, fatback, lard and beans had to come first. Then the house rent had to be paid; sometimes we had a little something extra."

A family of mill workers pose in their kitchen.
BETTMANN/CORBIS.

Estelle's home, like most mill-village houses, was small. Built in rows, houses in mill villages usually had five or six rooms, electric lights, and indoor kitchens. Sometimes families grew food in small gardens.

Many mill-village houses had no running water. Inside, families lived simply. Sometimes there would be a parlor with a family Bible, or pictures on the wall. Families tried to have good clothes for Sundays and holidays. Children went barefoot in the summer. Families ate pork, some chicken, and occasionally rabbits, squirrels, or quail. Diets included some fruits and vegetables: cabbage, corn in season, beans, potatoes, tomatoes, cucumbers, and onions, with fruit and berries for pies. But for many families the usual diet was unhealthy: fatback pork (meat that comes from a layer of fat that runs along the animal's back), beans, and cornbread, varied occasionally by eggs or chicken, with few or no vegetables.

Life was hard for most mill-village families, and children worked hard. As Estelle

A little girl working in a Southern mill. LIBRARY OF CONGRESS.

Berry recalled, "Young folks on a cotton mill hill ain't got much chance to enjoy themselves. . . . People as poor as us does well to make a living."

I'VE BEEN THERE EVER SINCE

Children began working in Southern mills at a young age. Mary Branch took a job at the Royal Cotton Mill in Wake Forest, North Carolina, when she was just eight years old. In 1938, she told an interviewer, "I've been there ever since and I'm sixty now."

Like most children, Mary turned her pay over to her parents for a long time. "Papa set me free when I was nineteen and after that what I made was mine," she said. After years of work, Mary managed to save $1,400. "Then the bank went busted and I lost my money."

Three girls eat their lunch in a mill. LIBRARY OF CONGRESS.

Emma Willis spent a lifetime in mills, from age twelve until seventy-five. "I worked in a cotton mill for sixty-three years, but I never did care for it much," Emma said when she was eighty-one.

In the beginning, Emma worked from six in the morning until seven at night, earning thirty-five cents a day. "Every pay day that come, I brought my money home and laid it in my mother's hand; then after she died, I turned every cent over to my sister who kept house for me almost fifty years. I worked steady, too, once while I was at the Cannon Mill I went eleven years without missing a

day's pay. Back then if you didn't go, they'd send for you because they didn't have anyone else to do your work."

Mrs. Albert Farlow had known hard work on her father's farm from the time she was a small girl. "I hoed corn and picked cotton from the time I was six years old," she said. When she was nine, she went to work in the mill at Milledgeville, North Carolina.

"I worked in the spinning room every day in the week, twelve hours a day. I was paid ten cents a day. . . . [T]he pay is better now, but the work is harder. Workin' in the mill now is just slavery."

When children started mill work, they often weren't put on the payroll right away — they had to learn the job first.

One of twelve children, Bertha Awford Black of Thomasville, North Carolina, was eleven when she took a job in a cotton mill. The girl who trained her was even younger.

"I stayed with her, her a-learnin' me, for about two weeks, and I didn't get anything for it," said Bertha. Once she had learned, she was given two spinning frames to work, earning twenty-five cents a day for twelve hours of work.

"After a few weeks' time I got to where I could run six sides. That was seventy-five cents a day and I drew nine dollars for a full pay day every two weeks. I'd take that money and I'd give it to our mother. We all did. . . . She always looked after us good," recalled Bertha.

Even though the hours were long, Bertha liked mill work and the steady wages it brought better than the uncertain life of farming. And at first, Bertha remembered, the mill owners kept up the houses "pretty good."

But Bertha regretted not being able to go to school. "You know, that ought to have been stopped a long time before it was," she reflected. "We didn't get any education. We weren't old enough to go to work. That child labor law was wonderful when it came about. We, every one, should have been in school."

LINT WOULD BLOW EVERYWHERE

In addition to long hours, working in the cotton mill was dangerous. Clara Thrift of Thomasville, North Carolina, reported, "At the time I didn't think my work was dangerous but looking back now I realize it was, breathing in all that lint. People were always getting hurt in some way, you know, getting your hand hurt or mashing your fingers.

"As far as fresh air, there wasn't any. . . . When the thread came from the spinning room, it had a lot of lint on it and when you would rewind it, the lint would blow all up in your nose, your ears, and your eyes," said Clara.

There was so much lint that Clara and other mill workers were often called "lint-heads." Cotton dust and lint in a person's lungs and eyes could also be dangerous, causing infection and disease. Exposure to cotton dust can cause byssinosis, or brown lung disease. Without unions or adequate protection, many mill workers suffered without being compensated.

Harsh supervisors made the job even more difficult, said Clara. They watched every move the workers made. "We were allowed to go to the bathroom but we had to run there and get right back. . . . You tried to go to the bathroom before and after work. You really didn't have time to go during work. . . . You could take ten minutes for lunch. You'd go get your lunch and come on back to your machine and eat while you worked."

Clara, like her mother, had always worked in the mill. "I didn't think much about it. I just thought about making the money to get me a house and to raise my kids so they would never have to do the things I've done. . . . All the women there felt the same way."

A boy works a warping machine in a Tennessee cotton mill. LIBRARY OF CONGRESS.

SOMETHING BETTER

Life was especially hard for mill workers in the 1930s, during the Great Depression, when millions lost their jobs. While many Northern mills closed, most Southern textile mills remained open. However, as mill owners tried to squeeze out as much profit as possible, mill workers found that their wages were cut or that they were expected to handle even more work and machines than before without getting any more money.

A family evicted from their home after cotton-mill strikes. BETTMANN/CORBIS.

The earnings of mill owners and managers were usually kept secret. Workers in some mills began to protest against unfairness and tried to organize unions, despite strong opposition to their efforts. In September 1934, the United Textile Workers helped organize a general strike among Southern mill workers. But the strike ended unsuccessfully after twenty-two days. In the aftermath, many working-class leaders found themselves laid off or threatened.

"We tried to return to our jobs . . . [but] we were met and turned back before we got to the mill," said one Ruby Mitchell, describing the armed men hired by mill officials to punish the union supporters.

"These past three years have been hard enough to make a body wonder if life is worth livin' at all," said Eunice Smith, a mill worker, in August of 1938. "There was several months when the five of us lived on as little as three dollars a week. When I'd have as much as three dollars at a time I'd buy a twenty-four pound sack of flour and a bucket of lard. We lived off of biscuit bread and what stuff I'd canned the summer before."

Mrs. Smith's hopes were on her daughter, Lusette, who had struggled to finish high school.

"Most people look back on their senior year as a pleasant time in their lives, but I won't," Lusette said. "I walked the three miles in to high school every morning because I didn't have money for bus fare. The walking wouldn't have been so bad if I hadn't been afraid each day that my ragged shoes would fall apart before I could possibly get to school.

"Then, too, walking in the early morning can make you awfully weary when you haven't had any breakfast and not much supper the night before," Lusette went on. It was hard for her to listen to classmates discuss their plans for the future. "I didn't talk any because I was afraid even to think what my future might be."

But Lusette felt determined to get a good job that would make her parents proud and allow her to help her little brothers so they would have happier memories of school than she had.

"Surely I can get a job on my own," Lusette said. "I'll have to, because I can't stand to live all my life at a cotton mill village."

COTTON PICKERS:
THE FORCES OF CHANGE

"Three of us pick. I'm twelve years old and my bag is twelve feet long. I can drag nearly a hundred pounds. My sister is ten years old, and her bag is eight feet long. My little brother is seven, and his bag is five feet long."

— YOUNG BOY COTTON PICKER

THE BOLL WEEVIL: THROUGH WITH COTTON

Walter Strange, a white farmer born in 1899 in South Carolina, began sharecropping when he was only twelve, asking for a plot of land from his neighbor, Mr. Kerningham.

"Son, you can't manage a farm," Mr. Kerningham replied.

But Walter begged, "Give me a chance."

Despite his young age, Walter was able to persuade the man to let him begin farming. As the years went by, through hard work and luck, Walter was able to move from sharecropping to being a tenant farmer. As a young man, he also married and started a family.

But Walter had another dream during the thirteen years he was a tenant farmer, renting his land from others. He wanted his own farm. At last, he managed to save enough money to look around for a place. "I bought it and made the first payment twenty-one years ago. By working hard and saving, doing without things we would have enjoyed, I finished paying for it in five years."

Children working in the cotton fields. LIBRARY OF CONGRESS.

A young man works as a sharecropper. LIBRARY OF CONGRESS.

Walter was proud of what he had accomplished. "Right here I raised my family of four boys and one girl. . . . I'm up in the morning at five, and I go all day, working till late."

By the time Walter told his life story in 1938, times had gotten hard. The Great Depression had struck the country. The soil on his farm was worn out. Not only that, an infestation of the boll weevil, an insect that attacks cotton, had begun to threaten all he'd worked so hard for.

"Last year I planted seven acres in cotton and made only one bale. I used poison, too. But the boll weevil ate up the cotton in spite of it," said Walter. "The fertilizer cost me one hundred dollars. I sold the cotton for fifty-two dollars. The loss on the fertilizer alone was forty-eight dollars, not counting the work and the other expense. I had to sell something else to finish paying for the fertilizer.

"I am through with cotton."

THE GREAT MIGRATION

Many changes took place in the South in the early twentieth century. African Americans had been leaving the South since Reconstruction, the period of transition following the Civil War. But in the early years of the twentieth century, so many blacks left for Northern cities, such as Chicago, New York, and Philadelphia, that the movement came to be called the Great Migration.

African Americans moved away from the South for complex reasons. They wanted to escape sharecropping, a system which kept families in a cycle of poverty and debt, as well as segregation and racial violence. Floods, natural disasters, lack of educational opportunities, and the infestation of the boll weevil also compelled many families to leave. While conditions pushed black families to leave, there was also the pull of new opportunities and higher wages in the North. World War I, which began in Europe in 1914 and which America entered in 1917, opened up jobs for blacks in Northern factories.

The migration of blacks to the North continued well into the twentieth century.

A family of sharecroppers rest on their front porch.
LIBRARY OF CONGRESS.

It's estimated that between 1916 and 1970, more than six million blacks left the South, bringing with them rich social, cultural, and musical traditions that were to have a profound effect on American politics, literature, and music in the twentieth century.

THE GREAT DEPRESSION

The Great Depression, which struck in the 1930s, also affected cotton farming and caused economic hardship for millions. Cotton farmers were already some of the poorest people in the nation. In 1929, the average American farm family earned $1,240, about a third of the average for non-farm families. The states that grew cotton often stood at the bottom of the list.

The Great Depression made conditions even more difficult for farmers like Walter Strange. The price of cotton dropped. Years of farming just one crop meant that the soil was worn out and depleted, and many farmers could not afford fertilizer. Infestations of the boll weevil also caused severe problems for farmers.

The drop in prices affected other people besides farmers. In Georgia, Joe Byrd had a business selling fertilizer, wagons, buggies, and other items. His wife explained, "The boll weevil also got in its deadly work. They practically destroyed the cotton and damaged other crops as well. Prices dropped so low that what little the farmers were able to salvage brought almost nothing and consequently they had no money with which to meet their obligations." Since her husband had extended credit to the farmers, when the Depression came, he was unable to collect. The result was, said Mrs. Byrd, "We lost our business and our home."

Many blacks had already left farms, migrating to cities, both north and south. White families still sharecropping were driven out by the Great Depression when the price of cotton dropped drastically. In 1929, a farmer could sell cotton at seventeen cents a pound. The next year it dropped to nine and a half cents, and in 1931, it hit five and a half cents, the lowest price since 1894.

Some tenant or sharecropping families who lost their toehold on the land became

A family of "gasoline gypsies" with their belongings piled into their truck. LIBRARY OF CONGRESS.

"gasoline gypsies," piling kids, tents, pots, pans, and other belongings into a car. Others traveled by wagons, by train, or by foot. In the years after the Civil War, cotton farming had been moving westward, taking hold in Texas and, finally, southern California. In the hard years of the Great Depression, many families from the South made their way westward, too, to the cotton fields in the Imperial Valley of California. They became migrant field-workers, hiring out their labor wherever they could find work.

These families set up camps and pitched their tents along the road, near the irrigation ditches. They got their drinking water from the ditches, rarely boiling it.

Children and parents worked from sunup until dark. Then the family would have a meal and go to sleep, exhausted. The next morning they would have to be ready for work again.

One mother, when asked how many hours her children worked in the field, explained, "As long as we could all hold out . . . from sunup to sundown." It was, she said, what they had to do to get something to eat.

In the fields, the sun beat down intensely. Cotton pickers had a loose strap of material at the opening of their bag. This was slipped over the child's head. The opening to the bag was at the waist, so that cotton could be dropped in, while the bag dragged behind.

Children in the fields were "thick as bees," said one school principal. "All kinds of children pick — even those as young as three years! Five-year-old children pick steadily all day."

Regulating child labor wasn't easy. The National Child Labor Committee, formed in 1904, had challenged the use of child labor in factories and sweatshops and promoted compulsory education for all children. But it wasn't until 1938, when the Fair Labor Standards Act was passed, that minimum ages of employment and hours of work for children were regulated by federal law.

Nevertheless, the laws were often difficult to enforce. While young children skipping school to work in the fields violated child labor and school attendance laws, most employers looked the other way.

A family picking cotton in the fields. LIBRARY OF CONGRESS.

Children went to school before and after the harvest. LIBRARY OF CONGRESS.

Said one school principal, "I am absolutely sure that employers know they are evading the state law. . . . They say it will ruin their business if children do not work."

"I sometimes pick till I have over a hundred pounds. I pick as long as I can pull the bag, and until it gets so heavy I can't walk straight."
— CHILD COTTON PICKER

THE END OF AN ERA

Cotton remained the chief crop in the South until around World War II. Eventually, the effects of the Great Depression and government policies in the 1930s led to the end of sharecropping and a transformation of Southern agriculture. Many small farms disappeared. For example, in 1940, there were an estimated 2.4 million farms in eleven Southern states; in 1974, there were 723,000 farms. Most were much larger and were run by businesses rather than families.

Still, picking cotton by hand continued in some places well into the mid-twentieth century. During the fall cotton harvest season in Arizona in the late 1940s and early 1950s, about two thousand black migrant cotton pickers arrived each week to pick cotton. In 1952, there were about fifty thousand workers picking cotton by hand in Arizona, and 70 percent of those were African Americans.

Cotton had always depended on the use of small tools and human labor. Other crops had already adapted easily to the use of machines. But handpicking cotton was cleaner, so some growers hesitated to use machines until the mid-1950s and early 1960s. It's not surprising, then, that cotton was among the last crops in America to be mechanized. Yet eventually, machines took over the planting and harvesting in most areas.

Working cotton had meant lives of toil and poverty for generations of Americans. As one historian concluded, "The poorest people suffered the most from the ever-spreading cultivation of cotton."

MILL WORKERS:
THE LAST GENERATION

"A lot of people came to Lowell because Lowell was supposed to be a big textile city. So they came from all over. Canada, Greece, Poland, and then we had the young ladies that used to live on the farms. They came to Lowell. Why? Not because they were forced to come to Lowell, they came to Lowell because they wanted to be somebody."

— HENRY PARADIS, 1984

LOWELL IN THE TWENTIETH CENTURY

Athena Theokas was just fourteen when she left her native Greece to come to America. In 1916, the boat trip across the gray, stormy Atlantic Ocean took twenty-four days.

Athena arrived in New York City alone, with twelve dollars in her pocket. She made her way by train to Lowell, Massachusetts, where relatives and friends from Greece had already settled. Soon she found a job spinning in the Merrimack Mill twelve hours a day, from six in the morning until six at night, earning about five dollars a week.

"Just like the others," said Athena Theokas when she shared her life story at the age of seventy-two, "I come to work."

————

A New England loom worker.
LIBRARY OF CONGRESS.

NEW IMMIGRANTS IN THE MILLS

Athena arrived in Lowell almost eighty-five years after young Lucy Larcom, and she was not alone. Lowell continued to draw workers to its mills in the late nineteenth and early twentieth centuries.

During the Civil War major investments had been made in building new textile mills in Lowell. Although the South became a competitive force in the early 1900s, the industry in New England continued to expand.

After the Civil War, while women from the North continued to come to work in the Lowell textile mills, thousands of supplemental or additional workers were needed, too. In the late 1870s, Lowell textile companies began recruiting French Canadians.

In addition to cotton cloth, factories made carpets, stockings, cotton and wool

A girl works at a machine in a New England mill. LIBRARY OF CONGRESS.

underwear, and the upholstery for furniture and train seats. Other mills produced thread, elastic, shoelaces, tapes, cords, suspenders, and ribbons. By the 1930s, most of the original Lowell textile companies had been sold; some retained the original names, and others operated under new names. There were eight thousand textile workers in Lowell.

Gradually the makeup of the textile-worker population changed. In the mid-1880s, Northern women made up half of the textile workforce in Lowell, while most of the others were French Canadian or Irish. According to the 1900 population census for Lowell, however, immigrants came from Canada and Ireland, as well as Great Britain, Greece, Portugal, Sweden, and Poland.

During the nineteenth- and early twentieth centuries the Lowell textile companies rebuilt their textile mills. Workers lived in nearby tenements and crowded worker housing facilities. By 1911, the seventy-three-hour work week common in 1839 had been reduced to fifty-four hours, six days a week. In 1938, workers began working the now-standard forty-hour week of eight hours each day, five days a week.

ROUGH AND GOOD

Several years after she arrived in Lowell, Athena Theokas married. She and her husband raised ten children during the 1930s, when America was plunged into the Great Depression.

"Staying alive, it takes a piece of work," Athena said of these hard times. Athena stayed home for some years to raise her children, earning a little extra money by crocheting and embroidering. She returned to work in the mills in 1941.

Although in the 1940s her pay had risen to fifteen dollars a week, Athena found little improvement in working conditions. The pressure on the mills to produce more goods at less cost meant, she said, that "they doubled the work of the people." If she worked ten machines at once, she was expected to work fifteen.

Life was especially hard with such a large family. Without a washing machine, just getting the family laundry done was backbreaking work.

"I used to wash by my hands and put the clothes outside at night. . . . No dryer, no washer, no nothing," Athena remembered. After being on her feet all day, Athena spent countless evenings drying clothes over the stove, and ironing them, so her children could have clean clothes to wear to school the next day.

Despite the hardships, Athena Theokas valued her fellow workers and neighbors. Mothers watched out for children; working people treated others like brothers and sisters. "Even very poor people, they work together and love each other, the neighbors never fight."

Looking back, Athena reflected, "So I don't know, my life it was . . . rough and good."

A HUNDRED PERCENT

Unlike immigrant Athena Theokas, Henry L. Paradis was born in Lowell, in 1918. His father, a French Canadian, had come to New England for the promise of steady work in the mills.

"By coming to Lowell . . . they could earn money, and maybe send their brother or sister to school," Henry explained. His father found a job and worked forty-eight years in the Suffolk Mills, "twelve hours a day, six days a week for five dollars and fifty cents a week."

When Henry reached the age of eighteen, he began to work in a mill, too. His first job was changing the bobbins on a hundred looms. "So I really had to move fast. I was young and strong and fast. In those days, it was good money, in an envelope on Thursday afternoon. And when you got home Thursday night you gave your mother your pay, unopened. That's a fact."

In his spare time, Henry learned to weave. When Henry told his boss about his new skill, he was offered a chance to weave on the late shift, from nine thirty at night until six in the morning. Henry never forgot that first nerve-racking night with new responsibilities.

"So Monday night I went to work. The boss says, O.K., these are your looms. Sixty looms. Now I knew how to weave, but I didn't have the experience of running sixty looms! So I started at nine thirty and I really worked hard all night. The night went by so fast, I didn't even see it."

Cotton workers judge the quality of cotton. LIBRARY OF CONGRESS.

Henry did well enough to keep his job as a weaver on the late shift, making eighteen dollars a week. But he wanted to keep learning, so he attended textile school during the day to learn loom fixing. "I didn't tell anybody, but when I graduated I walked in the mill and I said to my boss, here's my diploma — loom fixing," Henry recalled.

Much to Henry's surprise, his boss offered him not more money but less! He could start as a loom fixer at sixteen dollars a week. Henry was already making more than that. At last his boss offered nineteen dollars. Henry agreed, on one condition. "You'll give me twenty-one in a month."

A girl works at a loom drawing from rows of bobbins. LIBRARY OF CONGRESS.

Henry got his way. And just a few months later, when his supervisor died suddenly of a heart attack, Henry was asked to take over. Before long he had sixty-eight people working for him.

"I'm the type of a man that if I do something, I go all out," he declared at the age of sixty-six. "I have interest. A hundred percent interest."

THE END OF "KING COTTON" IN LOWELL

By the 1930s, "King Cotton" was limping along in Lowell. In 1940, there were still eight thousand textile workers in Lowell. In addition to Boott and the Merrimack Manufacturing Company, there were other large companies such as Shaw, Wannalancit, and Lawrence Manufacturing Company, along with many smaller companies.

Those textile companies that survived in Lowell did so as a result of diversification — producing high-end, quality fabrics. Many cotton mills closed during the Great Depression.

By 1950, Lowell's industry was made up of rayon manufacturing, shoe factories, garment-making shops, and electrical equipment manufacturers. The last two remaining cotton textile mills shut down in the mid-1950s.

Jean Rouses, who went to work in the mills after graduating from Lowell High School in 1947, witnessed the closing of the mills.

"The word went around that they were just going to close down and that's all there was to it. . . . It was sad," she said. "A lot of people . . . worked hard but they enjoyed their work. It was a kind of job that you took pride in. You worked hard but you took pride in it."

THE LAST GENERATION

Historian Mary Blewett arrived in Lowell in 1965. As she looked at the shabby city, with its hulking, mostly abandoned mills, vanishing ethnic neighborhoods, and decaying housing, she became curious about the lives of the last generation of mill workers, people who had survived hard economic times and labored for years in the mills.

She began to collect their life histories. She soon learned that the mill workers all shared one goal: "They never wanted to see their children at work in any mill."

Mary Rouses Karafelis (whose sister Jean Rouses and mother also worked in the mill), was part of this last generation. Graduating from Lowell High School in 1941, Mary couldn't find a job in an office. Her mother, Soultana Rouses, had come from Greece and had spent most of her life toiling in the mill. She wanted something different for her daughter.

After Soultana Rouses had helped settle a workers' dispute, the mill manager promised that if he could ever help her out, he would try. Her request was this: that he give Mary, her daughter, a chance to prove herself working in the mill's office.

The day after graduation, Mary went to see the manager, Mr. Flather. "I am giving you a job because your mother asked me to, but I want you to know that I am giving you three months to learn it. If you don't learn it in three months you will be fired."

Mary Karafelis started at sixteen dollars a week, working forty hours a week. Her job was in payroll. In those days, before computers, keypunch machines were used to print the checks. By the end of her first year, Mary had proved herself. She was running the whole payroll, over a million and a half dollars.

"I used to go up into the mills to have lunch with my mother because she worked up there. . . . I never saw anything like it. They had these big . . . wooden boxes that weighed a ton, that they had to fill with the bobbins and lift them themselves, women! Lifting them, to dump them into big bins. And not only that, the cotton, the lint in the air . . .

"It was hot, my God! A hundred forty degrees. . . . And I just thanked my mother every day."

Mary Karafelis understood the sacrifices her mother had made. Whether they were Northern women in the 1840s and 1880s or Greek and French Canadian immigrants in the 1890s and 1940s, workers toiled in the Lowell textile mills to improve the lives of their families. Like thousands of others, Soultana Rouses was able to accomplish her most deeply held dream: to give her children a chance at a better life.

A HUNDRED POUNDS OF COTTON: CHILDREN THEN AND NOW

The voices of children weave through the story of cotton. Whether they were slaves, the sons and daughters of sharecroppers, or mill workers, young people often felt the brunt of America's cotton culture throughout the nineteenth century and well into the twentieth.

One of these children was Shelby Kirk. Born in 1894, Shelby was the daughter of a North Carolina tenant farmer, who began working in the fields from the time she could walk. She never forgot the first time she picked one hundred pounds in a single day. "My daddy told me that if I picked a hundred pounds of cotton that day, he'd give me fifty cents. I picked a hundred pounds of cotton that day and the next day I couldn't walk I was so sore. I was thirteen years old, that was my birthday. I never will forget it. I kept that fifty cents so long."

It wasn't unusual for young children like Shelby to pick all day. Sometimes even toddlers worked in the fields. Theo Clark was just two years old in 1917 when he picked three pounds of cotton in one November afternoon. Before Inez Foley was big enough to drag a sack behind her, she was following behind her mother up and down the rows.

"I picked little piles of cotton and she'd come along and pick it up," said Inez. When she was ten, Inez got her own sack to drag along behind her.

Children head into a cotton field for work. LIBRARY OF CONGRESS.

Since children have small, nimble fingers, they often picked just as quickly as adults. But picking took its toll on small hands. Tullia Ischy, who lived in central Texas, described how hard it was to extract that bit of fluff out of its sharp casing.

"You had to pick every bit of it out of the burs. I hated to pull them old burs 'cause they hurt your hands. Even if you had on some gloves, they'd stick you anyhow. When they open up, there's a little point on every one of those at the edge of the burs." (The bur is the part of the plant that holds the cotton locks, or fluff, in place when it is ready to be picked.)

On early mornings, a chill, heavy dew made the cotton plants wet. The moisture made the children's hands soft, so the sharp points of the burs would cause them to bleed.

"But you kept on picking," said one child. "In a little while the sun might come up and drive the dew away, then the bur points would get sharper, but you kept on picking."

CHILDREN THEN . . .

Across the country, people concerned about child labor tried to improve conditions for children. In the late eighteenth century and early nineteenth century, reformers worked hard to pass laws to limit children's work in factories.

Despite the passage of the 1938 Fair Labor Standards Act regulating minimum ages of employment and work for young people, children continued to work in the fields. For instance, in 1940, one reformer estimated that "the number of children under 16 years working in agriculture at the present time is about 500,000. The 1940 Census showed 175,000 but did not take into account children under 14."

In 1940, a report from the Federal Children's Bureau stated that American children did jobs such as "thin, hoe, pull, and top sugar beets; weed cabbages and other vegetables; pull, top, and tie onions, radishes, and carrots; cut and bunch asparagus; gather string beans, lima beans, peas, tomatoes, walnuts, cranberries, strawberries, and other berries; pick prunes, some other orchard fruits, and hops; chop and pick cotton. Children of agricultural laborers also work in drying sheds at such processes as cutting fruits, such as peaches, apricots, and pears."

Cotton has been called the most important American crop. Between 1794, when Eli Whitney patented the saw gin, and World War II, cotton shaped the lives of generations of Americans — young and old, black, white, and Latino. Cotton played a key role in the plantation system, slavery, the sharecropping system, and the Industrial Revolution and growth of factories.

Although some people made money from cotton, the majority toiled in thankless, difficult jobs in fields and factories. Children often began working at early ages and never had opportunities to go to school. Growing the single crop of cotton left many totally dependent on cotton prices, and it also hurt the land and people's health. It's no wonder that cotton culture was sometimes called evil.

At one time, the Cotton Belt stretched across a swath of land 300 miles north to south, and 1,600 miles from the Carolinas to western Texas. More than a million acres were devoted to cotton. Slavery and cotton grew up together in the Old South. But year after year of planting cotton depleted the soil. And so cotton kept moving westward, keeping former slaves and white farmers in poverty through the sharecropping system. For a time the United States was the chief cotton-producing country in the world, eagerly providing a cheap textile to hungry markets all over the globe. Today, in addition to the United States, top cotton-producing countries include China, India, Pakistan, and Uzbekistan.

. . . AND CHILDREN NOW

Although young children in America don't labor in cotton fields and mills as they once did, harsh conditions for child workers still exist. In 2004, the International Labour Organization, a United Nations (UN) agency, estimated that about 246 million children in the world were child laborers, and some of these children work in cotton fields and mills.

For example, according to a 2004 report from the UN Office for the Coordination of Humanitarian Affairs, in Uzbekistan some children labor in cotton fields for ten hours or more a day, picking cotton instead of attending school during harvesttime.

It has also been reported that cotton mills in south India that employ young girls from nearby villages are becoming increasingly prevalent. In March 2004, a UN agency reported that children between the ages of six and fourteen make up 88 percent of the workforce producing cotton seeds in two districts in India. Primarily girls, these children often drop out of school to work full-time. Many children, the report states, wake before daybreak and work in the fields from five in the morning until six or seven at night.

The next time you buy clothes made of cotton, take time to look at the label. Consider doing some research to see what working conditions are like where that cloth was made. Or, at least, think of the boys, girls, men, and women in this book, and of the many, then and now, whose stories and voices are forgotten or unheard.

FURTHER READING FOR YOUNG PEOPLE

The books and resources listed below are just a sampling of the many wonderful picture books, nonfiction, and historical fiction about the cotton industry available for young readers.

Cotton Fields, Slavery and Plantation Life, Farmers

Erickson, Paul. *Daily Life on a Southern Plantation: 1853*. New York: Lodestar Books, 1997.

Lester, Julius, and Rod Brown (Illustrator). *From Slave Ship to Freedom Road*. New York: Dial Books, 1998.

L'Hommedieu, Arthur John. *From Plant to Blue Jeans: A Photo Essay*. New York: Scholastic Library Publishing, Children's Press, 1998.

McKissack, Patricia C. *A Picture of Freedom: The Diary of Clotee, a Slave Girl*. (Dear America) New York: Scholastic, 1997.

McKissack, Patricia C., Frederick McKissack, and John Thompson (Illustrator). *Christmas in the Big House, Christmas in the Quarters*. New York: Scholastic, 1994.

Robinet, Harriette Gillem, and Wendell Minor (Illustrator). *Forty Acres and Maybe a Mule*. New York: Atheneum, 1998.

Taylor, Mildred D. *Roll of Thunder, Hear My Cry*. New York: Puffin Books, 1976.

Williams, Sherley Anne, and Carole Byard (Illustrator). *Working Cotton*. New York: Harcourt Brace, 1992.

Cotton Mills and Workers

Bartoletti, Susan Campbell. *Kids on Strike!* New York: Houghton Mifflin, 1999.

Boling, Katharine. *January 1905*. New York: Harcourt Children's Books, 2004.

Denenberg, Barry. *So Far from Home: The Diary of Mary Driscoll, an Irish Mill Girl, Lowell, Massachusetts, 1847*. (Dear America) New York: Scholastic, 1997.

Freedman, Russell, and Lewis Hine (Photographer). *Kids at Work: Lewis Hine and the Crusade Against Child Labor*. New York: Clarion Books, 1994.

McCully, Emily Arnold. *The Bobbin Girl*. New York: Dial Books, 1996.

Paterson, Katherine. *Lyddie*. New York: Dutton Books, 1991.

Lowell National Historical Park Web site: http://www.nps.gov/lowe/2002/home.htm

Center for Lowell History, University of Massachusetts–Lowell Web site: http://library.uml.edu/clh/index.html

SELECTED BIBLIOGRAPHY

Books

Agee, James, and Walker Evans. *Let Us Now Praise Famous Men*. Boston: Houghton Mifflin, 1941.

Banks, Ann. *First-Person America*. New York: W. W. Norton & Company, 1991. (Originally published by Alfred A. Knopf, Inc., 1980.)

Berlin, Ira, Marc Favreau, and Steven F. Miller, eds. *Remembering Slavery: African Americans Talk About Their Personal Experiences of Slavery and Emancipation*. New York: The New Press, in association with the Library of Congress, 1998.

Blewett, Mary H. *The Last Generation: Work and Life in the Textile Mills of Lowell, Massachusetts, 1910-1960*. Amherst: University of Massachusetts Press, 1990.

Bruchey, Stuart, ed. *Cotton and the Growth of the American Economy: 1790-1860, Sources and Readings*. New York: Harcourt Brace & World, Inc., 1967.

Byerly, Victoria. *Hard Times Cotton Mill Girls: Personal Histories of Womanhood and Poverty in the South*. Ithaca: ILR Press, Cornell University, 1986.

Caldwell, Erskine, and Margaret Bourke-White. *You Have Seen Their Faces*. Athens and London: University of Georgia Press, 1995. (Originally published by Modern Age Books in 1937.)

Daniel, Pete. *Breaking the Land: The Transformation of Cotton, Tobacco, and Rice Cultures Since 1880*. Urbana and Chicago: University of Illinois Press, 1985.

Dodge, Bertha S. *Cotton: The Plant That Would Be King*. Austin: University of Texas Press, 1984.

Dublin, Thomas, ed. *Farm to Factory: Women's Letters, 1830-1860*, Second Edition. New York: Columbia University Press, 1993.

Federal Writers' Project. *These Are Our Lives*. New York: Arno Press, 1939.

Foley, Neil. *The White Scourge: Mexicans, Blacks, and Poor Whites in Texas Cotton Culture*. Berkeley: University of California Press, 1998.

Gibbons, Charles Edward. *Child Labor Among Cotton Growers of Texas: A Study of Children Living in Rural Communities in Six Counties in Texas*. New York: National Child Labor Committee, 1925.

Hall, Jacquelyn Dowd, ed.; James Leloudis, Robert Korstad, Mary Murphy, Lu Ann Jones, and Christopher B. Daly. *Like a Family: The Making of a Southern Cotton Mill World*. Chapel Hill and London: University of North Carolina Press, 1987.

Hearden, Patrick J. *Independence and Empire: The New South's Cotton Mill Campaign, 1865-1901*. DeKalb: Northern Illinois University Press, 1982.

Hirsch, Jerrold. *Portrait of America: A Cultural History of the Federal Writers' Project*. Chapel Hill: University of North Carolina Press, 2003.

Holley, Donald. *The Second Great Emancipation: The Mechanical Cotton Picker, Black Migration, and How They Shaped the Modern South*. Fayetteville: University of Arkansas Press, 2000.

Johnson, Charles Spurgeon, Edwin Embree, and W. W. Alexander. *The Collapse of Cotton Tenancy: Summary of Field Studies and Statistical Surveys, 1933-35*. Chapel Hill: University of North Carolina Press, 1935.

Lakwete, Angela. *Inventing the Cotton Gin: Machine and Myth in Antebellum America*. Baltimore and London: Johns Hopkins University Press, 2003.

Lankford, George E., ed. *Bearing Witness: Memories of Arkansas Slavery: Narratives from the 1930s WPA Collections*. Fayetteville: University of Arkansas Press, 2003.

Larcom, Lucy. *A New England Girlhood.* New York: Corinth Books, 1961. (Originally published in 1889.)

LeSeur, Geta. *Not All Okies Are White: The Lives of Black Cotton Pickers in Arizona.* Columbia and London: University of Missouri Press, 2000.

Maharidge, Dale, and Michael Williamson. *And Their Children After Them.* New York: Pantheon Books, 1989.

McCurry, Dan. C., ed. *Children in the Fields: American Farmers and the Rise of Agribusiness, Seeds of Struggle.* New York: Arno Press, 1975.

McNeilly, Donald P. *The Old South Frontier: Cotton Plantations and the Formation of Arkansas Society, 1819-1861.* Fayetteville: University of Arkansas Press, 2000.

Moran, William. *The Belles of New England: The Women of the Textile Mills and the Families Whose Wealth They Wove.* New York: St. Martin's Press, 2002.

Nelson, Lawrence J. *King Cotton's Advocate: Oscar G. Johnston and the New Deal.* Knoxville: University of Tennessee Press, 1999.

Robinson, Harriet Hanson. *Loom and Spindle, or Life Among the Early Mill Girls.* Kailua, Hawai'i: Press Pacifica, 1976. (Reprint of the 1898 edition.)

Rosengarten, Theodore. *All God's Dangers.* New York: Random House, 1974.

Scranton, Philip. *Proprietary Capitalism: The Textile Manufacture at Philadelphia, 1800-1855.* Philadelphia: Temple University Press, 1983.

Sharpless, Rebecca. *Fertile Ground, Narrow Choices: Women on Texas Cotton Farms, 1900-1940.* Chapel Hill: University of North Carolina Press, 1999.

Sitton, Thad, and Dan K. Utley. *From Can See to Can't: Texas Cotton Farmers on the Southern Prairies.* Austin: University of Texas Press, 1997.

Thompson, Holland. *From the Cotton Field to the Cotton Mill: A Study of the Industrial Transition in North Carolina.* Freeport, NY: Ayer Company Publishers, Inc., 1971. (Originally published by Macmillan, 1906.)

Whartenby, Franklee Gilbert. *Land and Labor Productivity in United States Cotton Production, 1800-1840.* New York: Arno Press, 1977.

Willoughby, Lynn. *Fair to Middlin': The Antebellum Cotton Trade of the Apalachicola/Chattahoochee River Valley.* Tuscaloosa and London: University of Alabama Press, 1993.

Woodman, Harold D. *King Cotton and His Retainers: Financing and Marketing the Cotton Crop of the South, 1800-1925.* Columbia: University of South Carolina Press, 1990.

Articles, Oral Histories, Narratives, Bulletins, and Pamphlets

American Life Histories: Manuscripts from the Federal Writers' Project, 1936-1940. Library of Congress. Accessed through American Memory. http://memory.loc.gov/ammem/

The Child Labor Bulletin: "Child Labor and Poverty," vol. 2, no. 1 (May 1913). New York: National Child Labor Committee, 1913.

Hughes, Louis. *Thirty Years a Slave: From Bondage to Freedom. The Institution of Slavery as Seen on the Plantation and in the Home of the Planter.* Milwaukee: South Side Printing Company, 1897. Electronic edition scanned by University of North Carolina at Chapel Hill Libraries, *Documenting the American South.* http://docsouth.unc.edu/hughes/hughes.html

McKelway, Alexander Jeffrey. *Child Wages in the Cotton Mills: Our Modern Feudalism.* New York City: National Child Labor Committee Pamphlet no. 199, 1913. (Originally published: *The Child Labor Bulletin,* vol. 2, no. 1 [May

1913]). Electronic edition scanned by University of North Carolina at Chapel Hill Libraries, *Documenting the American South*.
http://docsouth.unc.edu/nc/mckelway/mckelway.html

U.S. Department of Labor, Children's Bureau. *The Welfare of Children in Cotton-Growing Areas of Texas*. Bureau publication no. 134. Washington, D.C.: Government Printing Office, 1924.

Williams, James. *Narrative of James Williams, An American Slave, Who Was for Several Years a Driver on a Cotton Plantation in Alabama*. New York: American Anti-Slavery Society, 1838. Electronic edition scanned by University of North Carolina at Chapel Hill Libraries, *Documenting the American South*.
http://docsouth.unc.edu/williams/williams.html

NOTES

INTRODUCTION
Unraveling the Threads

p. 1 "I remember hearing . . .": Henry Kirk Miller, *Born in Slavery: Slave Narratives from the Federal Writers' Project, Arkansas Narratives*, vol. 2, pt. 5, Library of Congress, pp. 78-79.

PART I

p. 5 "All hail to the great king . . .": "King Cotton," Baltimore, 1 January 1862, *Civil War Song Sheets Collection*, Rare Book and Special Collections Division, Library of Congress, Digital ID cw200950.

CHAPTER ONE
A Shoeful of Cotton Seeds

p. 7 "Before they ever had a [cotton] gin . . .": Paul Smith, *Born in Slavery: Slave Narratives from the Federal Writers' Project, 1936-1938, Georgia Narratives*, vol. 4, pt. 3, Library of Congress, p. 324.

new colony of Virginia: Angela Lakwete, *Inventing the Cotton Gin: Machine and Myth in Antebellum America* (Baltimore and London: Johns Hopkins University Press, 2003), p. 22.

single most important ingredient: Lynn Willoughby, *Fair to Middlin': The Antebellum Cotton Trade of the Apalachicola/Chattahoochee River Valley* (Tuscaloosa and London: University of Alabama Press, 1993), p. 4.

cotton was grown for export: Lakwete, *Inventing the Cotton Gin*, p. 23.

p. 8 "putting out system": Lowell National Historical Park, "The Industrial Revolution in England," Lowell National Historical Park Handbook, p. 140.

pp. 9-10 English textile manufacturing: Chris Aspin, *The Cotton Industry* (Buckinghamshire: Shire Publications Ltd., 2004), pp. 11-12.

p. 10 "mule": Aspin, Ibid., p. 13.

p. 11 In 1765, about a half million pounds of cotton: John Steele Gordon, "King Cotton," *American Heritage*, vol. 43, no. 5 (September 1992), p. 18.

English textile industry need for cotton: Lowell National Historical Park Handbook, p. 140.

history of cotton: Lakwete, *Inventing the Cotton Gin*, pp. 2-20.

cotton species today: Ibid., pp. 2-3.

p. 12 "The task set for them . . .": Mrs. Cicero Russell Range-Lore, *American Life Histories: Manuscripts from the Federal Writers' Project, 1936-1940*, American Memory, Library of Congress, Manuscript Division, WPA Federal Writers' Project Collection, p. 1.

p. 13 cotton gin history: Lakwete, *Inventing the Cotton Gin*, pp. 1-6.

In the 1770s . . . roller gins: Ibid., pp. 22-23.

"Those home-made cotton gins . . .": Smith, *Born in Slavery*, p. 324.

Eli Whitney's new gin: Lakwete, *Inventing the Cotton Gin*, p. 48.

CHAPTER TWO
Up Before Daybreak: Cotton and Slavery

p. 17 "Everybody had to get up . . .": Richard Orford, *Born in Slavery: Slave Narratives from the Federal Writers' Project, 1936-1938, Georgia Narratives*, vol. 4, pt. 3, Library of Congress, p. 149.

"I sure have had . . .": Ira Berlin, Marc Favreau, and Steven F. Miller, eds., *Remembering Slavery: African Americans Talk About Their Personal Experiences of Slavery and Emancipation* (New York: The New Press, in association with the Library of Congress, 1998), p. 73.

"Old Master strapped us . . .": Ibid.

p. 18 "I had to card and spin . . .": Ibid., p. 75.

p. 19 slavery built cotton empire: Ibid., p. xxxi.

cotton the most important export: Willoughby, *Fair to Middlin'*, p. 1.

p. 20 three million enslaved: Berlin, *Remembering Slavery*, p. xxxi.

p. 21 "Even before it was light . . .": Orford, *Born in Slavery*, pp. 149–150.

"Even us kids . . .": John Walton, *Born in Slavery: Slave Narratives from the Federal Writers' Project, 1936–1938, Texas Narratives*, vol. 16, pt. 4, Library of Congress, p. 125.

"Along about the first of March . . .": Smith, *Born in Slavery*, p. 323.

p. 22 "Of course we lived . . .": David Wilborn, *The African-American Experience in Ohio, 1850–1920*, Works Progress Administration Ex-Slave Narratives, Ohio Historical Center Archives Library, American Memory, Library of Congress, p. 1.

"ride up and down . . .": Walton, *Born in Slavery*, pp. 1–2.

p. 23 "I never knew . . .": Hannah Scott, *Born in Slavery: Slave Narratives from the Federal Writers' Project, 1936–1938, Texas Narratives*, vol. 16, pt. 4, Library of Congress, p. 6.

"was mean . . .": Ibid., p. 7.

"I carried the bucket . . .": Ibid.

"When I got bigger . . .": Ibid, pp. 7–8.

p. 24 "Old Bat wouldn't let us go. . . .": Ibid.

"He thought . . .": Ibid., p. 8.

owners moved slaves to Texas: Rebecca Sharpless, e-mail correspondence, 17 March 2005.

CHAPTER THREE
Mountains of Cotton

p. 27 "It must be seen . . .": Harold D. Woodman, *King Cotton and His Retainers: Financing and Marketing the Cotton Crop of the South, 1800–1925* (Columbia: University of South Carolina Press, 1990), pp. vii–viii.

"I have worked . . .": James Johnson, *Born in Slavery: Slave Narratives from the Federal Writers' Project, 1936–1938, South Carolina Narratives*, vol. 14, pt. 3, Library of Congress, p. 42.

p. 29 boat landings and wharves: Willoughby, *Fair to Middlin'*, p. 19.

p. 30 most cotton was shipped: Ibid., p. 14.

cotton bales exported: Ibid.

Warehouses overflowed: David Black, "Cotton and Horseshoes," *American Life Histories: Manuscripts from the Federal Writers' Project, 1936–1940*, Library of Congress, Manuscript Division, WPA Federal Writers' Project Collection, p. 4.

Cotton was the life: Ibid, p. 5.

cotton exports to Great Britain: Stuart Bruchey, ed., *Cotton and the Growth of the American Economy: 1790–1860, Sources and Readings* (New York: Harcourt Brace & World, Inc., 1967), pp. 14–16.

river systems: Willoughby, *Fair to Middlin'*, pp. 30–31.

planter John W. Brown and his cotton factor: Woodman, *King Cotton*, pp. 32–40.

pp. 30–31 Mr. Henderson's duties: Ibid., p. 39.

p. 32 John Chrystie: Willoughby, *Fair to Middlin'*, pp. 100–102.

"We have . . .": Ibid., p. 101.

John Chrystie was very busy: Ibid.

"A place must be selected . . .": Black, "Cotton and Horseshoes," p. 2.

p. 33 cotton colors: Willoughby, *Fair to Middlin'*, p. 22.

"We put the samples . . .": Ibid., p. 23 (from the Barrow Papers, Southern Historical Collection, 5 March 1859).

"booming down the river . . .": Ibid., p. 100 (from the *Apalachicola Commercial Advertiser*, 30 September 1844).

ships entered Apalachicola Bay: Ibid., pp. 33–34.

CHAPTER FOUR
At the Clang of a Bell: The Mill Girls of Lowell

p. 37 "I shall not stay here. . . .": William Moran, *The Belles of New England: The Women of the Textile Mills and the Families Whose Wealth They Wove* (New York: St. Martin's Press, 2002), p. xi.

p. 38 earliest memories: Lucy Larcom, *A New England Girlhood* (1889; reprint New York: Corinth Books, 1961), pp. 46–47, 107–108.

"gobblings": Ibid., p. 124.

when Lucy's father died: Ibid., p. 116.

p. 39 Lucy hated to leave: Ibid., p. 147.

"In the sweet June weather . . .": Ibid., pp. 182–183.

p. 40 Samuel Slater's mill: Moran, *The Belles of New England*, p. 51.

p. 41 Re-invention of power loom: "Lowell," Lowell National Historical Park pamphlet, National Park Service, U.S. Department of the Interior.

Francis Cabot Lowell: Benita Eisler, ed., *The Lowell Offering* (New York: W. W. Norton & Company, 1977), p. 13.

build a new city: "Lowell," Lowell National Historical Park pamphlet.

new textile mills would . . .: Thomas Dublin, ed., *Farm to Factory: Women's Letters, 1830-1860* (New York: Columbia University Press, 1993), p. 6.

p. 42 "city of the future . . .": Moran, *The Belles of New England*, p. 15.

named the city Lowell: Ibid., pp. 52–55.

p. 43 "something better . . .": Ibid., p. 5.

New England girls: Ibid., p. 3.

mill worker statistics in 1840s: Dublin, *Farm to Factory*, pp. 5-6; e-mail correspondence with Martha Mayo, Director, Center for Lowell History, University of Massachusetts-Lowell, March 2005.

p. 44 women's wages in 1830s: Ibid., pp. 10–12.

pp. 44-45 Lucy at home and mill: Larcom, *A New England Girlhood*, pp. 150-154.

p. 45 "It really was not hard . . .": Ibid., pp. 153–154.

"The buzzing and hissing . . .": Ibid., p. 154.

"It was so huge . . .": Ibid.

"But alas! . . .": Ibid., pp. 155–156.

"The mill itself . . .": Ibid., p. 155.

p. 46 pasted poems in mill: Ibid., pp. 175–176.

p. 47 "The Improvement Circle": Ibid., p. 174.

self-improvement clubs: Eisler, *The Lowell Offering*, p. 33.

history of *Lowell Offering*: Ibid., pp. 33–38.

Laura Nichols: Moran, *The Belles of New England*, pp. 8–9.

pp. 47–49 Lowell workers demographics: Martha Mayo, e-mail correspondence, March 2005.

p. 49 mill girls' activism: Moran, *The Belles of New England*, p. 8.

"pioneers in the struggle . . .": Ibid., p. 2.

PART II

p. 51 " 'Next year . . .' ": Woodman, *King Cotton*, p. 313 (from E. E. Miller, "The Cropper Speaks," as reprinted from *The Forum*, in Clarence Poe, "The Farmer and His Future," W. T. Couch, ed., *Culture in the South* [Chapel Hill, University of North Carolina Press, 1934, p. 323]).

CHAPTER FIVE
From Can to Can't: Sharecroppers and Tenant Farmers

p. 53 "Picking goes on . . .": James Agee and Walker Evans, *Let Us Now Praise Famous Men* (Boston: Houghton Mifflin, 1941), p. 340.

world's cotton supply: Bruchey, *Cotton and the Growth of the American Economy*, p. 7.

number of plantations: Ibid., p. 21.

pp. 55-56 post-Civil War South: Woodman, *King Cotton*, pp. 245–253.

p. 56 sharecropping system took hold: Rebecca Sharpless, *Fertile Ground, Narrow Choices: Women on Texas Cotton Farms, 1900-1940* (Chapel Hill: The University of North Carolina Press, 1999), p. 7.

p. 57 "You go up to a man . . .": Ambus Gray, *Born in Slavery: Slave Narratives from the Federal Writers' Project, 1936-1938*, Library of Congress, Manuscript Division, p. 78.

"about all you got . . .": Ibid., pp. 78–79.

p. 58 borrowing to get by: Sharpless, *Fertile Ground, Narrow Choices*, p. 11.

"All of a sudden . . .": Theodore Rosengarten, *All God's Dangers* (New York: Vintage Books, 1974), pp. 17–18.

"just a lump of blood . . .": Ibid., p. 18.

"What did I have left? . . .": Ibid., p. 108.

pp. 58–59 "You ain't got sense . . .": Ibid., p. 109.

p. 59 "ain't goin' to let me rise . . .": Ibid., p. 108.

"My house is so rotten . . .": Charles Johnson, Edwin Embree, and W. Alexander, *The Collapse of Cotton Tenancy: Summary of Field Studies and Statistical Surveys, 1933-35* (Chapel Hill: University of North Carolina Press, 1935), p. 16.

"has no ceiling . . .": Neil Foley, *The White Scourge: Mexicans, Blacks, and Poor Whites in Texas Cotton Culture* (Berkeley: University of California Press, 1998), p. 81.

"unpainted weather-beaten houses . . .": Sharpless, *Fertile Ground, Narrow Choices*, pp. 87–88.

Manuel Longoria: Foley, *The White Scourge*, p. 81.

pp. 59–60 "We can't get . . .": Johnson, *Collapse of Cotton Tenancy*, p. 18.

p. 60 cotton families in rural Texas: Sharpless, *Fertile Ground, Narrow Choices*, pp. 88–95.

p. 61 "three M's": Johnson, *Collapse of Cotton Tenancy*, p. 17.

p. 63 "I had to fix lunch . . .": Thad Sitton and Dan K. Utley, *From Can See to Can't: Texas Cotton Farmers on the Southern Prairies* (Austin: University of Texas Press, 1997), p. 122.

"I had to be boy and girl . . .": Jacquelyn Dowd Hall, ed., et al., *Like a Family: The Making of a Southern Cotton Mill World* (Chapel Hill and London: University of North Carolina Press, 1987), p. 17.

"I've sure had to work . . .": George Tanner, *American Life Histories: Manuscripts from the Federal Writers' Project, 1936-1940*, Library of Congress, Manuscript Division, WPA Federal Writers' Project Collection, p. 3.

"I don't remember . . .": Ibid., p. 4.

p. 64 children's use of wages: Dan C. McCurry, ed., *Children in the Fields: American Farmers and the Rise of Agribusiness, Seeds of Struggle* (New York: Arno Press, 1975), pp. 27–29.

p. 65 Missouri school ranking: Ibid., p. 10.

"Most of the local people . . .": Ibid., p. 6.

"miserable panorama . . .": Johnson, *Collapse of Cotton Tenancy*, p. 14.

"The tenant farmer . . .": Erskine Caldwell and Margaret Bourke-White, *You Have Seen Their Faces* (1937; reprint Athens and London: University of Georgia Press, 1995), p. 6.

CHAPTER SIX

They Called Us Lintheads: Mill Villages of the South

p. 67 "If we don't starve . . .": Dave McCarn, "Cotton Mill Colic," American folk song.

Flossie Durham: Hall, *Like a Family*, p. 34.

"We lived . . .": Ibid.

p. 68 Piedmont mills: Ibid., p. 26.

p. 69 "Things had got tough . . .": Ibid., p. 41.

"We thought it was easier . . .": Ibid.

John Wesley Snipes: Ibid., pp. 41–42.

moving from farms to mill villages: Ibid., p. 33.

p. 70 "As soon as the Depression . . .": Ibid., p. 42.

"public work": Ibid., p. 44.

"Long hours . . .": Jerrold and Karen Hirsch, "Disability in the Family?: New Questions about the Southern Mill Village," *Journal of Social History* 35.4 (2002), pp. 919–933.

p. 71 blacks in Southern mills: Hall, *Like a Family*, pp. 66–67.

"This man come down . . .": Victoria Byerly, *Hard Times Cotton Mill Girls: Personal Histories of Womanhood and Poverty in the South* (Ithaca: ILR Press, Cornell University, 1986), pp. 128–129.

"I was born . . .": Estelle Berry, *American Life Histories: Manuscripts from the Federal Writers' Project, 1936-1940*, Library of Congress, Manuscript Division, WPA Federal Writers' Project Collection, p. 1.

p. 72 "put on a clean frock . . .": Ibid., p. 2.

p. 73 mill families' diet: Hall, *Like a Family*, pp. 149–150.

p. 74 "Young folks . . .": Berry, *American Life Histories*, p. 2.

"I've been there ever since...": "Description of a Mill Village," *American Life Histories: Manuscripts from the Federal Writers' Project, 1936–1940,* Library of Congress, Manuscript Division, WPA Federal Writers' Project Collection, p. 6.

"Papa set me free...": Ibid.

"I worked...": Emma Willis, *American Life Histories: Manuscripts from the Federal Writers' Project, 1936–1940,* Library of Congress, Manuscript Division, WPA Federal Writers' Project Collection, p. 1.

"Every pay day...": Ibid., p. 5.

p. 75 "I hoed corn...": Mrs. Albert Farlow, *American Life Histories: Manuscripts from the Federal Writers' Project, 1936–1940,* Library of Congress, Manuscript Division, WPA Federal Writers' Project Collection, p. 5.

"I worked in the spinning room...": Ibid.

p. 76 "I stayed with her...": Byerly, *Hard Times Cotton Mill Girls,* p. 62.

"After a few weeks' time...": Ibid., p. 66.

"pretty good...": Ibid.

"You know...": Ibid., p. 65.

"At the time...": Ibid., pp. 116–118.

brown lung: Hall, *Like a Family,* p. 81.

p. 77 "We were allowed...": Byerly, *Hard Times Cotton Mill Girls,* p. 120.

"I didn't think...": Ibid., p. 117.

mill workers in Great Depression: Hall, *Like a Family,* p. 319.

p. 78 "We tried to return...": Ibid., p. 351.

p. 79 "These past three years...": Eunice Smith, *American Life Histories: Manuscripts from the Federal Writers' Project, 1936–1940,* Library of Congress, Manuscript Division, WPA Federal Writers' Project Collection, p. 15.

"Most people look back...": Ibid., p. 17.

"Surely I can get a job...": Ibid., p. 18.

CHAPTER SEVEN

Cotton Pickers: The Forces of Change

p. 81 "Three of us pick....": McCurry, *Children in the Fields,* p. 250.

"Son, you can't manage...": Walter Strange, *American Life Histories: Manuscripts from the Federal Writers' Project, 1936–1940,* Library of Congress, Manuscript Division, WPA Federal Writers' Project Collection, p. 4.

"Give me a chance.": Ibid.

"I bought it...": Ibid., p. 8.

p. 82 "Right here I raised...": Ibid.

"Last year I planted...": Ibid., p. 11.

p. 84 American farm families in 1929: Johnson, *Collapse of Cotton Tenancy,* pp. 1–11.

"The boll weevil...": Mrs. J. R. Byrd, *American Life Histories: Manuscripts from the Federal Writers' Project, 1936–1940,* Library of Congress, Manuscript Division, WPA Federal Writers' Project Collection, p. 7.

driven out by Great Depression: Johnson, *Collapse of Cotton Tenancy,* pp. 46–63.

p. 85 cotton farming moves west: Ibid., p. 3.

Imperial Valley: McCurry, "California the Golden," *Children in the Fields,* pp. 233–236.

p. 86 "As long as we could all hold out...": Ibid., p. 6.

"thick as bees...": Ibid., p. 236.

p. 88 "I am absolutely sure...": Ibid., p. 242.

"I sometimes pick...": McCurry, *Children in the Fields,* p. 250.

p. 89 farms, 1940 and 1974: Sitton, *From Can See to Can't,* p. 2.

cotton pickers in Arizona: Geta LeSeur, *Not All Okies Are White: The Lives of Black Cotton Pickers in Arizona* (Columbia and London: University of Missouri Press, 2000), p. 102.

In 1952...: Ibid., pp. 107–108.

handpicking cotton: Ibid., p. 110.

mechanization of cotton farming: Johnson, *The Collapse of Cotton Tenancy,* p. 41.

"The poorest people . . .": Sharpless, *Fertile Ground, Narrow Choices*, p. 122.

CHAPTER EIGHT

Mill Workers: The Last Generation

p. 91 "A lot of people . . .": Mary H. Blewett, *The Mill Workers of Lowell Oral History Project*, Lowell National Historical Park, interview with Henry Paradis, 1984, p. 1.

"Just like the others . . .": Ibid., pp. 1–2.

pp. 92–93 Lowell mills: Mary H. Blewett, *The Last Generation: Work and Life in the Textile Mills of Lowell, Massachusetts, 1910-1960* (Amherst: University of Massachusetts Press, 1990), pp. 3–5.

p. 93 textile-worker population: Ibid., pp. 3–8.

Lowell mills in the twentieth century: Martha Mayo, e-mail correspondence, April 2005.

"Staying alive . . .": Blewett, *Mill Workers of Lowell*, interview with Athena Theokas, p. 4.

"they doubled the work . . .": Ibid., p. 7.

p. 94 "I used to wash . . .": Ibid., p. 13.

"Even very poor people . . .": Ibid., p. 9.

"So I don't know . . .": Ibid.

"By coming to Lowell . . .": Blewett, *Mill Workers of Lowell*, Paradis, p. 1.

"twelve hours a day . . .": Ibid., p. 2.

"So I really had to move fast. . . .": Ibid.

p. 95 "So Monday night . . .": Ibid., p. 3.

p. 96 "I didn't tell anybody . . .": Ibid.

"You'll give me . . .": Ibid.

p. 97 "I'm the type of a man . . .": Ibid., p. 9.

decline of cotton mills in Lowell: Blewett, *The Last Generation*, pp. 7–8.

Lowell in the 1950s: Ibid., p. 8.

"The word went around . . .": Blewett, *Mill Workers of Lowell*, interview with Jean Rouses, 18 February 1985, p. 13.

p. 98 "They never wanted . . .": Blewett, *The Last Generation*, p. 8.

"I am giving you a job . . .": Ibid., p. 311.

"I used to go . . .": Blewett, *Mill Workers of Lowell*, interview with Mary Rouses Karafelis, 26 February 1985, p. 5.

CONCLUSION

A Hundred Pounds of Cotton: Children Then and Now

p. 101 "My daddy told me . . .": Byerly, *Hard Times Cotton Mill Girls*, p. 128.

"I picked little piles . . .": Sharpless, *Fertile Ground, Narrow Choices*, p. 177.

p. 102 "You had to pick . . .": Ibid., p. 179.

"But you kept on picking. . . .": Ibid.

"the number of children . . .": McCurry, "Children Who Work on the Nation's Crops," *Children in the Fields*, p. 8.

"thin, hoe, pull . . .": Ibid., p. 7.

p. 103 Cotton Belt: Johnson, *Collapse of Cotton Tenancy*, p. 2.

p. 104 UN Office for the Coordination of Humanitarian Affairs 2004 report: IRIN News.org, "Uzbekistan: Focus on Child Labour in Southern Cotton Sector." http://www.plusnews.org. Accessed 5 February 2005.

international mills: "South Indian Workers in Dire Straits, says NGO," *One World Asia*. Accessed December 2004. "Asia Child Rights, A Comprehensive Portal on Asia Child Rights from the Asia Human Rights Commission," *ACR Weekly Newsletter*, vol. 3, no. 49, 8 December 2004. http://acr.hrschool.org/mainfile. php/0175/300/

child labor: International Programme on the Elimination of Child Labour, Safety and Health Fact Sheet, Hazardous Child Labour in Agriculture (March 2004), ILO, Geneva, Switzerland. http://www.ilo.org.

TEXT PERMISSIONS

Every effort has been made to trace the ownership of any copyrighted material in this book and to secure permission from holders of the copyright. If there are questions, the publisher will include corrections and additions in subsequent editions. We gratefully acknowledge permission to quote from the following sources: • Excerpts from *All God's Dangers* by Theodore Rosengarten (New York: Random House, 1974) used by permission of Random House, Inc. • Excerpts from *Let Us Now Praise Famous Men* by James Agee and Walker Evans. Copyright © 1941 by James Agee and Walker Evans. Copyright © Renewed 1969 by Mia Fritsh Agee and Walker Evans. Reprinted by permission of Houghton Mifflin Company. All rights reserved. • Excerpts from *Hard Times Cotton Mill Girls: Personal Histories of Womanhood and Poverty in the South* by Victoria Byerly. Copyright © 1986 by Cornell University. Used by permission of the publisher, Cornell University Press. • Excerpts from *The White Scourge: Mexicans, Blacks, and Poor Whites in Texas Cotton Culture* by Neil Foley. Copyright © 1997 by The Regents of the University of California. Used by permission of the University of California Press. • Excerpts from *Fertile Ground, Narrow Choices, Women on Texas Cotton Farms, 1900-1940* by Rebecca Sharpless (Chapel Hill: The University of North Carolina Press, 1999) used by permission of the University of North Carolina Press. • Excerpts from *The Collapse of Cotton Tenancy: Summary of Field Studies and Statistical Surveys, 1933-35* by Charles Spurgeon Johnson, Edwin Embree, and W. W. Alexander (Chapel Hill: The University of North Carolina Press, 1935) used by permission of the University of North Carolina Press. • Excerpts from *Like a Family, The Making of a Southern Cotton Mill World* by Jacquelyn Dowd Hall, James Leloudis, Robert Korstad, Mary Murphy, Lu Ann Jones, Christopher B. Daly (Chapel Hill and London: The University of North Carolina Press, 1987) used by permission of the University of North Carolina Press. • Excerpts from "Disability in the Family?: New Questions about the Southern Mill Village," by Jerrold Hirsch and Karen Hirsch, Journal of Social History 35.4 (2002), 919–933, used by permission of George Mason University. • Excerpts from interview with Athena Theokas by Lewis Karabatsos, 1974. Oral History Collection — University of Massachusetts-Lowell, Center for Lowell History, used by permission. • Excerpts from interviews with Henry Paradis and Jean Rouses, The Mill Workers of Lowell Oral History Project, Lowell National Historical Park, used by permission. • Excerpts from *The Last Generation: Work and Life in the Textile Mills of Lowell, Massachusetts, 1910-1960*, by Mary H. Blewett. Copyright © 1990 by the University of Massachusetts Press, used by permission.

PHOTO CREDITS

Pages ii–iii, from left to right: Library of Congress, Reproduction no. LC-USZ62-83927. Library of Congress, Reproduction no. LC-US34-006345D. Library of Congress, Reproduction no. LC-USF34-009819-E. American Textile History Museum, Lowell, MA. American Textile History Museum, Lowell, MA. Library of Congress, Reproduction no. LC-USF33-011507-M4. • Page viii: American Textile History Museum, Lowell, MA. • Page 4: Library of Congress, Reproduction no. D4-16272. • Page 6: American Textile History Museum, Lowell, MA. • Page 8: Library of Congress, Reproduction no. LC-USZ62-64405. • Page 10: Library of Congress, 8846, Reproduction no. G612-T01-17984. • Page 12: American Textile History Museum, Lowell, MA. • Page 14: Library of Congress, Reproduction no. LC-USZ62-103801. • Page 16: The Granger Collection, New York, NY. • Page 18: Sarah Gudger, age 121, *Born in Slavery: Slave Narratives from the Federal Writers' Project 1936–1938*, Library of Congress Manuscript Division, Washington, D.C. 20540 [digital ID mesnp 111350]. http://memory.loc.gov/cgi-bin/query/D?mesnbib:1:. /temp/~ammem_FWts::. • Page 19: Library of Congress, Reproduction no. LC-USZ61-1423. • Page 20: Library of Congress, Reproduction no. LC-USZ62-89498. • Page 22: Library of Congress, Reproduction no. LC-USZ62-120433. • Page 24: Library of Congress, Reproduction no. LC-USZ62-76385. • Page 26: R.E.L. Wilson Photograph Collection, Butler Center for Arkansas Studies, Central Arkansas Library System, Little Rock, Arkansas. • Page 27: Library of Congress, Reproduction no. LC-D418-8148. • Page 28: Library of Congress, Reproduction no. LC-D4-19456. • Page 29: Library of Congress, Reproduction no. LC-D418-8121. • Page 31: Library of Congress, Call no. LOT 12693, no. 8. • Page 34: Library of Congress, Reproduction no. LC-D4-39533. • Page 36: American Textile History Museum, Lowell, MA. • Page 38: Courtesy of the Peabody Essex Museum. • Page 39: American Textile History Museum, Lowell, MA. • Page 41: American Textile History Museum, Lowell, MA. • Page 42: American Textile History Museum, Lowell, MA. • Page 43: Baker Library, Harvard Business School. • Page 44: American Textile History Museum, Lowell, MA. • Page 46: American Textile History Museum, Lowell, MA. • Page 48: American Textile History Museum, Lowell, MA. • Page 50: Library of Congress, Reproduction no. USF34-44560-D. • Page 52: Getty Images, New York, NY. • Page 54: Bettmann/Corbis, New York, NY. • Page 55: Library of Congress, Reproduction no. LC-USZ62-51248. • Page 57: Library of Congress, Reproduction no. LC-USF33-011507-M4. • Page 60: Library of Congress, Reproduction no. LC-USZ62-77112. • Page 61: Library of Congress, Reproduction no. LC-USF34-080062-D. • Page 62: Library of Congress, Reproduction no. LC-USZ62-83927. • Page 64: Library of Congress, Reproduction no. LC-USZ62-115400. • Page 66: Library of Congress, Reproduction no. LC-USZ62-74048. • Page 68: Library of Congress, Reproduction no. LC-USZ62-96800. • Page 70: Library of Congress, Reproduction no. LC-USZ62-86967. • Page 71: Library of Congress, Reproduction no. LC-USZ6-1234. • Page 72: Bettmann/Corbis, New York, NY. • Page 73: Library of Congress, Reproduction no. LC-USZ62-38564. • Page 74: Library of Congress, Reproduction no. LC-USZ62-121889. • Page 75: Library of Congress, Reproduction no. LC-USZ62-130784. • Page 77: Library of Congress, Reproduction no. LC-USZ62-96801. • Page 78: Bettmann/Corbis, New York, NY. • Page 80: Library of Congress, Reproduction no. LC-USF34-006345D. • Page 82: Library of Congress, Reproduction no. LC-USZ62-131189. • Page 83: Library of Congress, Reproduction no. LC-USF34-009819-E. • Page 85: Library of Congress, Reproduction no. LC-USZ62-85400. • Page 86: Library of Congress, Reproduction no. LC-USF34-001621-C. • Page 87: Library of Congress, Reproduction no. LC-USF33-030526-M4 DLC. • Page 88: Library of Congress, Reproduction no. LC-USF34-0552286-D. • Page 90: Library of Congress, Reproduction no. LC-USZ62-96302. • Page 92: Library of Congress, Reproduction no. LC-USZ62-65669 • Page 95: Library of Congress, Reproduction no. LC-USF34-052554-D. • Page 96: Library of Congress, Reproduction no. LC-USF346-042553-D. • Page 100: Library of Congress, Reproduction no. LC-USF34-051919-D.

INDEX